ISBN 978-1-331-31142-3
PIBN 10172711

English
Français
Deutsche
Italiano
Español
Português

www.forgottenbooks.com

Mythology Photography **Fiction**
Fishing Christianity **Art** Cooking
Essays Buddhism Freemasonry
Medicine **Biology** Music **Ancient**
Egypt Evolution Carpentry Physics
Dance Geology **Mathematics** Fitness
Shakespeare **Folklore** Yoga Marketing
Confidence Immortality Biographies
Poetry **Psychology** Witchcraft
Electronics Chemistry History **Law**
Accounting **Philosophy** Anthropology
Alchemy Drama Quantum Mechanics
Atheism Sexual Health **Ancient History**
Entrepreneurship Languages Sport
Paleontology Needlework Islam
Metaphysics Investment Archaeology
Parenting Statistics Criminology
Motivational

grace of God" is but the echo of the ancient boast of these royal robbers, "King by divine birth."

All the races of earth have been despoiled by "divinely begotten" despots and saviors, upheld by "divinely inspired" creeds. The Druids were expecting their god Esus, to whom they offered maidens in sacrifice, to beget a god, when along came the Christians with one already begotten. This satisfied the Druids, and they accepted Christianity. This is another proof of the truth of Christianity.

In accepting, with the approval of Rome, all the virgin births of deities he could find among the legends of Asia, the Abbe Orsini exclaims: "No, it is not by chance that the mystery of the incarnation of a God in the womb of a virgin is one of the fundamental doctrines of Asia. It is not by chance that the privileged women who bear in their womb that emanation of the Divinity are always chaste, beautiful and holy."

The gods have always not only chosen as mates the chaste and holy, but also the most charming of the daughters of men.

The divinely inspired Abbe Orsini, like the divinely inspired apocryphal Gospel of the Nativity of Mary, differs with the divinely inspired Abbe Boullan regarding the age and health of St. Joseph at the time of his marriage to the mother of God. The Abbe Orsini declares that the earthly husband of the Virgin was "a man of advanced age, a decayed patrician," and that it was on account of his infirmities that he was selected by the holy priests.

Considering the neutral part that this saint was destined to play in the divine comedy the "advanced age" and "decayed" story does seem the more reasonable.

The faithful, however, should have no difficulty in accepting both accounts.

The beautiful Mary, we are told, had many admirers who were neither old nor decayed. One of these, says the Roman Catholic "History of Carmel," named Agabus, "a young and wealthy patrician," became brokenhearted at the sight of Mary's marriage to the decrepit and decayed Joseph, and renounced his riches and went and dwelt in a cave. After the birth of Christ he became a Christian monk, and thereby saved his soul. Thus does Jehovah reward the faithful.

In prostituting the simple message of human brotherhood and peace into a religion to suit the ruling classes, the priests of the creed of Constantine have experienced considerable difficulty in removing the odium, in the eyes of the powers that be, as found in the early account of Jesus' lowly origin. The Abbe Orsini, in order to awe the masses and tickle the ears of princes, says: "Now, Joseph, although poor, was of the Davidical race. The blood of twenty kings flowed in his veins. * * * The holy daughter of Joachim did not lower herself, therefore, as much as might be thought by espousing the carpenter." Mary, be it remembered, was, according to the church, also of royal blood. Christ was therefore, according to the creed of Constantine, not only of divine heavenly blood, but also of royal earthly blood. He would be eligible to marry into the royal families were he living

chenor

THE EMPEROR CONSTANTINE

The Creed of Constantine;
Or the World Needs
a New Religion

By Lord

HENRY M. TICHENOR,

Author of The Life and Exploits
of Jehovah

Published by
PHIL WAGNER,
Pontiac Building,
St. Louis, Mo.

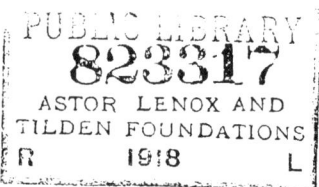

Copyright 1916

By

Phil Wagner

115

I Look Far Down the Reddened Road

I look far down the reddened road that reaches 'round the
    earth,
All strewn along with mangled men, and ask, What is it
    worth?
The ones that have been idolized as though surpassing
    great—
What are they worth—what glory marks these lauded
    lords of state?
What of the empires that are built on beds of dead men's
    bones—
What of the piles of princely pomp—the palaces and
    thrones—
What of the plunderers' proud power, and all their blood-
    bought things—
The curse and infamy of war—the pageantry of kings?

Such stuff as this is worthless trash to build a better
    world—
Far wiser that from every throne the last crowned king
    were hurled!
With none to blow the bugle blast to call the dogs of war,
Who, then, would march to murder those they never met
    before?
And all the retinue of priests, that say their God ordains

The crown that rests upon the brow of every brute that
    reigns—
Let these go, too, and take their myths, their goblins and
    their hell,
And give this tortured world of ours a longed-for breath-
    ing spell!

One peasant lad that plows the field where grows the
    golden corn,
Is nobler breed than all the whelps that wolves of war
    have borne;
One song sung by some genial soul, along some sheltered
    glade,
Shall hush some day the savage shock that madmen's
    guns have made;
One gleam of love that suckling babe in mother's eyes
    beheld,
Shall silence all the threats of doom that insane priests
    have yelled;
One word of brotherhood and peace—one breath from
    fragrant flowers—
These be the only things of worth, in this old world of
    ours!

THE tradition of a once Golden Age has been almost universal. The race memory of a time when the earth was owned in common has, through all the various social systems that have cursed mankind with class-rule, painted pictures of happy days when the world was young.

Of the tradition of those days Ovid has sung:
"The Golden Age was first, when man, yet new,
No rule but uncorrupted reason knew,
And, with a native bent did good pursue.
Unforced by punishment, unawed by fear,
His words were simple, and his soul sincere;
Needless was written law where none oppressed;
The law of man was written in his breast;
No suppliant crowds before the judge appeared,
No court erected yet, nor cause was heard,
But all was safe; for conscience was their guard.

*   *   *   *

No walls were yet, nor fence, nor moat, nor mound,
Nor drum was heard, nor trumpet's angry sound;
Nor swords were forged; but, void of care and crime,
The soft creation slept away their time."

Jupiter of the Greeks and Jehovah of the Jews were unknown. The priests that conceived them had not appeared. The jealous Juno had not given birth to Vulcan, the chariot builder, and Mars, the God of War. Osiris, son of Niobe and Jupiter, had not conquered

Egypt and enslaved the dark children of the Nile, to the power and glory of the Pharaohs. Baal and Moloch held no tyrant on the throne of Babylon, and Ormuzd had not crowned the princes of Persia. Brahma had not outraged India with castes, and Odin had not sent the swift Valkyries on phantom steeds to bring the souls of slaughtered warriors to Valhalla. Esus, God of the Druids, demanded no feasts of virgins' blood, the Christians' promises and threats had not been proclaimed, and there were no plutocrats to pick people's pockets. And all the sons and daughters of men loved and labored and played, in the Golden Age, that is told in the ancient legends, when the world was young; when friendly fairies lurked among the leaves and vines and flowers, and laughing woodnymphs danced beneath the spreading oaks with shifting shadows of the midnight moon.

It is a beautiful dream of a long ago, a passionate vision of the native love and longing of the race.

Then came the time of which the poet mourns: when
"The landmarks limited to each his right,
Where all before was common as the light."

The patriarch had arrived. The landlord loomed up. The master-class materialized. And these brought their paid priests with them. And these paid priests produced gods and goblins to hold the people in bondage. With promises of heaven and threats of hell the chains were forged. The earthly lord sat on a gilded throne by the grace of a sky lord who sat on a greater gilded throne.

A dream of a Golden Age when the world was young. A Dream—and a Prophecy.

THE CREED OF CONSTANTINE

THE prophet of Christendom is not the gentle Jesus; neither is the gospel of brotherhood and peace the Christian creed. The prophet of Christendom is the Emperor Constantine, and the Christian creed is the decision of the First Council of Nice.

This council, held under the auspices and authority of Constantine, repudiated the human Jesus, and created in his stead the mythical Christ; it changed the day of worship from the Jewish Sabbath (Saturday) to the pagan Sunday; it decreed the doctrine of eternal torture; it ordained the holy days and ceremonies, the sacred rites and festivals, all in accordance with Roman mythology; it gave us the Trinity—the three gods in one; and it gathered together the legends and fables that three centuries of illiterate "holy fathers" had conceived and written, and from this mass of myths selected and formed the New Testament.

Says so conservative a writer as Dean Dudley:

"In regard to the Canons and Decrees: I think the

best time for the Easter Festival would have been the ancient, honored day of the Jewish Passover. It was opposed merely by a whim of Constantine, because, as a Roman, he hated the nation which his country had long detested and persecuted, that is, the Jews. * * * His change in the Day of Rest arose from the same unjust prejudice."

Again says this writer:

"Whether Jesus taught the doctrine of an eternal hell for punishment in the after life, is a question among doctors of divinity. Origen denied it. The Roman Catholic Church has adopted purgatory in imitation of sheol, hades or tartarus. That church has many doctrines, forms and rites similar to those of the older religions. Jesus seems to have considered doing good deeds and living a pure life the true way to worship God" (Life of Constantine).

Even the Roman Catholic Church has never been quite brutal enough to consign souls immediately to a hell-fire. It provides an intermediate state from which they can be rescued. Protestantism alone promulgates the doctrine of immediate and eternal and hopeless damnation.

Of the religious ideas of Constantine, Dean Dudley writes: "His superstition was equal to his cunning. He praised and patronized the monks, nuns, hermits and devotees of every sort who deprived themselves of the comforts of life and despised nearly all social obligations. To live in rags and dirt, and eat herbs like some beasts was the holiest fashion in the estimation of the early

Fathers. They could not have deduced it from the life of Christ."

In order to prove his partnership with God and an assurance of a welcome entrance into heaven, Constantine had a gold coin struck with a likeness of himself on one side, and on the other a representation of his being transported to heaven, Elijah-like, in a chariot drawn by celestial steeds, with God's hand reaching down to receive him.

Constantine, like Napoleon, was a warrior—that is, he was a human butcher by profession. He usurped the throne and was proclaimed Emperor by his troops in the year 306. In the same year, in the city of Rome, Maxentius was proclaimed Emperor. Therefore, in order to hold the throne, Constantine felt compelled to kill Maxentius. This he did at the battle of the Milvian Bridge, in the year 312. Then Constantine, in order to make himself still more secure, put to death the two sons of Maxentius.

And herein is found the story of Constantine's conversion to Christianity.

The Emperor Maxentius adhered to the old religion of Rome and worshiped the pagan gods. "He was a vile tyrant," says Milman, "but not a persecutor." Roman paganism was becoming weaker and weaker. The real message of Jesus—the vision of equality and fraternity and peace—was still a menace to the empire. Then it was that the cunning of Constantine arose to the occasion. He became a Christian. He justified his slaughter of Maxentius and his two sons in the name of the Christian God, in order that a "true believer" might reign. Eusebius, who became a friend and flatterer of Constantine, thus records Constantine's "miraculous" conversion —conveniently occurring at the time that he was seeking justification in the eyes of the populace for the destruction of the Emperor Maxentius:

"Accordingly," says Eusebius, "he (Constantine) called on him (the Christian God), with earnest prayer and supplications, that he would reveal to him who he was, and stretch forth his right hand to help him in his present difficulties. And, while he was thus praying with fervent entreaty, a most marvelous sign appeared to him from heaven, the account of which it might have been difficult to receive with credit, had it been related by any other person. But since the victorious emperor himself, long afterwards, declared it to the writer of this history, when he was honored with his acquaintance and society, and confirmed his statement by an oath, who could hesitate to credit the relation, especially since the testimony of after-time (meaning, doubtless, Constantine's 'pious' life) has established its truth? He said that about midday, when the sun was beginning to decline, he saw with his own eyes the trophy of a cross of light in the heavens, above the sun, and bearing the inscription: 'IN HOC SIGNO VINCES!' (Under this sign thou shalt conquer.)

"At this sight he himself was struck with amazement, and his whole army also, which happened to be following him on some expedition, and witnessed the miracle.

"He moreover said that he doubted within himself what the import of this apparition could be. And while he continued to ponder and reason on its meaning, night imperceptibly drew on; and in his sleep the Christ of God appeared to him with the same sign which he had seen in the heavens, and commanded him to procure a standard made in the likeness of that sign, and to use it as a safeguard in all engagements with his enemies.

"At dawn he set his artificers to work and had the signal made and beautified with gold and gems. The Romans now call it the 'Labarum.' It was in the following form: A long spear overlaid with gold, crossed by a piece, laid over it. On the top of all was a crown, formed of gold and jewels interwoven, on which were placed two letters indicating the name of Christ—the Greek letter P being intersected by X exactly in its center. From the transverse piece, which crossed the spear, was suspended a banner of purple cloth covered with profuse embroidery of bright jewels and gold. It was of square form, and over it (beneath the cross) was placed a golden half-length picture of the emperor and his children. The standard he ordered to be carried at the head of all his armies."

Eusebius further states that Constantine told him that those who carried this standard never received a wound; that Christ himself went continually with it into battle. These and other wonderful things were claimed for the standard of Constantine.

It will be noted that all this was told to Eusebius by Constantine "long after" the miracle had happened. Eusebius is not the only holy father who has professed faith in such miraculous tales. Besides, Constantine was a powerful ruler, whose friendship was to be highly prized. And had it not been recorded that the Apostle Paul—who was repudiated by the first followers of Jesus —declared that it is right to lie to the glory of God? Paul, who, it is said, had also claimed to have seen a vision similar to Constantine's, and from hearing which Constantine had probably received his inspiration, had in his epistles emasculated the teachings of Jesus, as contained in the Sermon on the Mount—the only authentic words we have, as acknowledged by scholars, that fell from the lips of Jesus—and who carried the revolutionary message of the simple Jewish carpenter to a realm beyond the grave, had already set a foundation for the cunning work of Constantine. Moreover, Constantine was a pious and prayerful man, and that carries great weight. So it is easy to understand how Eusebius "believed" his story—or at least pretended to do so.

Constantine's purpose—his conspiracy—as plainly revealed in the work of the Council of Nice, was to create a creed, in the name of Christianity, that would be as acceptable to the ruling class as the ancient Roman mythology that was fast falling to pieces. It seems ridiculous to claim that Constantine himself really believed the new religion. His predecessors, the Roman emperors, as well as the educated patricians, only looked upon religion as a power to hold the masses in subjection; and the shrewdness and deceit employed by the tools of Constantine at the Council of Nice in formulating the "orthodox belief" of Christendom, and in compiling the "divinely inspired" New Testament to sustain them, discloses that no change of heart had taken place in this respect.

Christianity emerged from that Council as a combina-tion of Roman paganism and Old Testament savagery. The Jewish Jehovah was discovered to be even a more ferocious deity than any of the Roman gods. He was, therefore, doctored up a bit in order to make him still more bloodthirsty and vindictive—was made the father of a son to be offered to himself in sacrifice—the human Jesus with his message of fraternity and freedom and peace was transformed into a pagan myth, the promise of heaven for believers and the threat of hell for heretics was pronounced, and Constantine and his bishops doubt-less laughed in their sleeves at the crafty plot they had put across.

There is evidence that the early prelates of the church did not believe their own creed—that it was only intended for the masses. Faith, on the part of the rulers and the "upper" classes, came with the continued repetition of the story through the future years. The monks, the nuns, the lower orders of priests, and the ignorant people— these were the only ones at first supposed to be credulous enough to accept orthodox Christianity. The purpose of the Council of Nice, as conceived by Constantine, was to inaugurate a religion that would emphasize Paul's injunc-tion, "Servants, be obedient to them that are your mas-ters." Thus the popes and princes might live in splendor. And it worked—and is still working. Wallowing in wealth and surrounded with every luxury, Pope Leo X exclaimed, "And all these privileges have been secured to us by the fable of Jesus Christ" (Ernst Haeckel, Riddle of the Universe).

Such was the faith of the holy fathers who were posted.

The character of Constantine himself, the founder of the Christianity masquerading in the name of Jesus, was so unspeakably bestial that no rational person will credit him with either honesty or decency of purpose. He was a monster. Claiming the guidance of the god that slaughtered the Midianites, men, women and children, and turned the maidens over to the lust of the soldiers, Constantine murdered all who stood in his way, or who dared oppose his authority. He was a shining example for the war lords of Europe, and the coal barons—the butchers of Ludlow—of America, to follow, all of whom piously profess his religion. He murdered his wife, Fausta— had her suffocated in a boiling bath—and he murdered his father, Maximian; he murdered his own son, Crispus; he murdered Licinius, who had married his sister, and also her eleven-year-old child; these, and many more, did the Christian Emperor Constantine murder, many of whom were his own blood relations. And after every butchery he would rig himself in his royal raiment and sing, "Who is like to Thee, O Lord, among the gods?"

How like the rulers and exploiters of today!

Constantine had his likeness stamped on gold coins, with his eyes uplifted, as though in prayer. He destroyed the images of the pagan gods, and built churches all over the empire. His subjects were commanded to cease worshiping Jupiter and Diana and Apollo, and instead to worship Jehovah and the Virgin Mary and Christ.

The ignorant masses never knew the difference.

The theology of Constantine should even astonish some of the modern divines. He proved the virgin birth of Christ by quoting Virgil:

"Begin, Sicilian Muse, a loftier strain,
The voice of Cuma's oracle is heard again.

See where the circling years new blessings bring;
The virgin comes, and He, the long-wished king."

The best that can be said of Constantine is that, like most of "royal" blood, he was insane. He knew enough to be cunning and cruel, and that was all. His instincts were on a level with that of a gorilla. Philostorgius says that he murdered two wives, and that his three sons that survived him were the children of a prostitute. Such was the creature that convened and presided over the First Council of Nice, that gave us the doctrine of the Trinity, the Atonement, and the promise of heaven and threat of hell.

Roman society at that time, and up to the fall of the empire, was the vilest and most cruel imaginable; vile and cruel on the part of the aristocracy, and ignorant and slavish on the part of the impoverished masses. Continual wars had produced a race of degenerates. The immoralities and crimes against nature that were openly practiced at the feasts of the nobility are considered unprint-

able.   The description that Gibbon originally gave of
these feasts has been expurgated from his works by the
American authorities.

Thus does vulgar prudery cover over the social diseases that the great historian wisely pictured as a warning example.

There was no religious faith on the part of the ruling
class.   The gods of Rome and Greece, and the gods of
Egypt and Palestine, all looked alike to the Roman patricians.   They were all myths.   Among the educated there
were a few followers of the Greek school of philosophy—
a leaven, that, perhaps, had it not been destroyed by the
priests of Roman Christianity, might have saved the
decaying society.   But none of the educated formed any
part of the "holy fathers" chosen by Constantine to sit
in council and formulate the creed of Christendom. These
"holy fathers" were ignorant, drunken and licentious
priests.   They were politicians of the lowest type first,
and priests afterwards.   Such was the beginning of the
Roman Church; such it still is in its political machina-
tions.   Of these "religious" councils, that have given us
our "holy" and "inspired" creed, Bronson C. Keeler, in
his "History of the Bible," writes, quoting such authorities as Dr. Philip Schaff and H. H. Milman:

"The reader would err greatly did he suppose that in
these assemblies one or two hundred gentlemen sat down
to discuss quietly and dignifiedly the questions which had
come up before them for settlement.   On the contrary,
many of the bishops were ruffians, and were followed by
crowds of vicious supporters, who stood ready on the

slightest excuse to maim and kill their opponents. The most shocking scenes that occur in the ward political conventions in the worst districts of our great cities are as nothing compared with what history tells us was common in these Christian councils."

The First Council of Nice, upon whose decisions hang the faith of Christendom, was composed of priests who had barely stepped out of the myths of ancient pagan worship, and who decided "holy" questions by a knockdown fight or a vote. It is doubtful if any one of these clericals, who have told us all about our gods, devils, hell and damnation, drew a sober breath during the entire proceedings.

At the third general council of the Church, which was held at Ephesus in the year 431, history tells us that the "holy fathers" "came with armed escorts, as if going to battle, and were followed by great mobs of the ignorant rabble, slaves and seamen, the lower populace of Constantinople, peasants and bathmen, and hordes of women, prepared for violence." They "fought in the streets and much blood was shed." (Milman, History Latin Christianity.)

The true followers of the teachings of Jesus—those whom Ernst Haeckel historically describes as "communists, sometimes Social Democrats who, according to the prevailing theory in Germany today, ought to have been exterminated with fire and sword," were well nigh wiped out of existence by persecution, torture and martyrdom. In their stead had arisen a time-serving priesthood, followers of Paul, the Pharisee, instead of Jesus, the peasant. These priests had written innumerable gospels and epistles, to which they had affixed the names of early apostles. In these spurious writings Roman mythology played a much larger part than Judaism. The deism of Judaism was discarded, and the doctrine of the three gods taught. There was one sect, the Arians, followers of Arius, who still virtually denied the divinity of Jesus; but they were doomed to extinction before the power of Rome, that enunciated the savage story of a god begetting a son by a virgin, only to have him slaughtered in a bloody sacrifice to save sinners. And it was to make a binding state religion, with its salvation and damnation, its bloody sacrifice of Jesus and its trinity of deities, to deny which was not only blasphemy but treason, and to canonize a so-called New Testament, taken from the innumerable gospels and epistles that had accumulated during three centuries, that the First Council of Nice was convened by the Emperor Constantine.

Of the success of this council, Dean Dudley writes:

"The objects were all attained by the means of the Council, except the principal one. Arianism (that denied the divine birth of Jesus), though checked for a short time, again burst forth with ten-fold energy, and long agitated the religious world. However, it finally was completely vanquished and eradicated from the high places of Christendom."

As gleaned from history, it would be a spectacle to even stagger the faith of the most bigoted to view the make-up and proceedings of the First Council of Nice. Call to your mind an assemblage of 318 of the most ignorant, illiterate, cunning ward-heelers that has ever come to your notice; the Council of Nice was far more ignorant, and more illiterate, and more cunning than these. It was an age so degenerate that it was already fit to plunge itself into the abyss of the Dark Ages. Presiding over these 318 priests, sat the coarse, bloated-faced Constantine, the murderer. Such was the Council of Nice, inspired of God to canonize a holy scripture and proclaim a religion that damns to eternal torture those who deny it.

The way the work was done was something marvelous. Haeckel has given the following description of it in his "Riddle of the Universe":

"As to the four canonical gospels, we now know that they were selected from a host of contradictory and forged manuscripts of the first three centuries by the three hundred and eighteen bishops who assembled at the Council of Nice in 325. The entire list of gospels numbered forty; the canonical list contains four. As the contending and mutually abusive bishops could not agree about the choice, they determined to leave the selection to a miracle. They put all the books (according to the 'Synodicon of Pappus') together underneath the altar, and prayed that the apocryphal books, of human origin, might remain there, and the genuine, inspired books might be miraculously placed on the table of the Lord! The three synoptic gospels (Matthew, Mark, and Luke—all written 'after' them, not 'by' them, at the beginning of the second century) and the very different fourth gospel (ostensibly 'after' John, written about the middle of the second century) leaped on the table, and were thence-forth recognized as the inspired (with their thousand mutual contradictions) foundations of Christian doctrine. * * * The most important sources after the gospels are the fourteen separate (and generally forged) epistles of Paul. The genuine Pauline gospels (three in number, according to recent criticism—to the Romans, Galatians, and Corinthians) were written *before* the canonical gos-pels, and contain less incredible miraculous matter than they."

Thus started the Roman creed of Constantine on its cunning career.

CHAPTER II

"AFTER the extinction of paganism," writes Gibbon, "the Christians in peace and piety might have enjoyed their solitary triumph. But the principle of discord was alive in their bosom, and they were more solicitous to explore the nature, than to practice the laws, of their founder. * * * The disputes of the Trinity were succeeded by those of the Incarnation."

The mathematical riddle of three gods in one at first puzzled the minds of pagans who, with all their various gods and goddesses, gave a corporeal individuality to each deity; and the idea of a virgin conceiving by an incorporeal ghost somewhat strained their imagination.

The church became divided into two factions, one under the Patriarch of Constantinople, and the other under the Pope of Rome; and this division, in the Greek Catholic and Roman Catholic, still appears. Both, however, brandished the club that makes the creed of Constantine the most powerful—and the most contemptible—religion the ruling classes ever used to hold the slaves in submission: The threat of eternal and unspeakable torture to all who deny it.

The Gnostics apologized for the savage teaching of the universal damnation of the race, and the subsequent salvation of a select few through the bloody sacrifice of Jesus, by declaring that Jehovah of the Jews, who had damned the race, was a powerful demon, and that Jesus was a benevolent god that had come to earth to overturn the power of Jehovah. Not until the sixth or seventh century was the creed of Constantine, as it now exists, generally accepted; and the world first had to become a madhouse, through four centuries of dark ages, to firmly plant this creed in human brains.

Christianity, dating from the fourth century, can be best described as a joke and a tragedy—a joke, so far as the ruling classes were concerned, and a tragedy upon the part of the ignorant masses that believed it.

To a large extent this is true even to this day.

The church was divided into what Gibbon describes as "the Vulgar and Ascetic Christians." "The prince or magistrate, the soldier or merchant, reconciled their fervent zeal, and implicit faith, with the exercise of their profession, the pursuit of their interest, and the indulgence of their passions; but the Ascetics, who obeyed and abused the rigid precepts of the gospel, were inspired by the savage enthusiasm which represents man as a criminal, and God as a tyrant." They "embraced a life of misery, as the price of eternal happiness."

In other words, the creed of Constantine was not taken seriously by the nobility and professional classes, the soldiers and merchants; to them it was, in the language of Pope Leo X, "the fable of Jesus Christ." The purpose and mission of the creed of Constantine was to keep the masses in ignorance, superstition and servility. And it has faithfully fulfilled its intended purpose and mission. None but blind believers would have submitted to the exploitation and tyranny of the master classes, and have fought their wars, as the masses of Christendom have done for more than fifteen centuries.

The degradation to which some of the followers of the creed of Constantine voluntarily sunk themselves discloses the effect of orthodox Christianity on weak minds. Orders of Hermits, Monks, Anchorets, Nuns and other like lunatics overran the country. These renounced the world, chastised their bodies, mortified the natural instincts, abjured marriage, starved themselves, lived in dens and deserts, in cloisters and caves, scratched their skins raw with rough, sackcloth garments, wore pebbles in their shoes and thistles under their hairy shirts, and chanted dismal psalms to a wrathful deity in the hope of finally saving their souls from hell and obtaining a front seat in heaven. It was in the brains of such as these that miracles and monstrosities were conceived.

Now and then, in the triumphal march of this creed, appeared a man who had neither gone insane or renounced his integrity. These were hounded as heretics. They were tortured with every agony that the priests could conceive. They were burned at the stake and flayed alive. There is no infamy imaginable that Christianity cannot boast.

In the latter part of the sixth century there appeared in Arabia a "prophet" whose faith, at one time, threatened to wipe the creed of Constantine off the earth. Born in the city of Mecca, about the year 570, Mahomet from his early youth was a religious fanatic. "He sprung from the tribe of Koreish and the family of Hashem," records Gibbon, "the most illustrious of the Arabs, the princes of Mecca, and the hereditary guardians of the Caaba (the holy temple at Mecca). * * * In his early infancy he was deprived of his father, his mother, and his grandfather; his uncles were strong and numerous; and, in the division of the inheritance, the orphan's share was reduced to five camels and an Ethiopian maid servant. * * * According to the tradition of his companions, Mahomet was distinguished by the beauty of his person, an outward gift which is seldom despised, except by those to whom it has been refused. Before he spoke, the orator engaged on his side the affections of a public or private audience. They applauded his commanding presence, his majestic aspect, his piercing eye, his gracious smile, his flowing beard, his countenance that painted every sensation of the soul, and his gestures that enforced each expression of the tongue. * * * With these powers of eloquence, Mahomet was an illiterate Barbarian; his youth had never been instructed in the arts of reading and writing."

Such, in brief, is a description of the Prophet of Islam, who, by the sword, set out to bring the world back to the "one only and true God." That he could neither read or write was no reproach at that period. Few, even among the "upper" classes possessed this knowledge.

Professional scribes performed these services for pay, just as professional stenographers take dictation today.

Mahomet, in his religious zeal, looked into the prevailing religions around him—the newly invented creed of Constantne, and the ancient worship of the Jews. Neither suited him. He criticised the creed of Constantine on account of its trinity of gods, and he criticised the Jews for not accepting Jesus as a prophet sent from God. Nor did Mahomet admire the future reward that the creed of Constantine promised to believers. Singing bands of sexless angels with harps and crowns offered no attraction to the sensuous sons of the desert. So Mahomet pictured a Paradise abounding in beautiful black-eyed maidens, called *houris,* seventy-two of whom became the brides of the meanest of the faithful. To the Arabs this looked far more tempting than the promise of a gold crown and harp.

In his twenty-fifth year Mahomet married a rich widow of Mecca, named Cadijah, who embraced his religion and looked upon him as a prophet of God. After that the love affairs of Mahomet would doubtless have paralleled Solomon's had his means held out.

The angel Gabriel appeared to Mahomet with the information that the scriptures had been badly corrupted by different writers, and that God had chosen him to re-write them. From time to time Gabriel dictated to Mahomet as to what should be written; and Mahomet in turn dictated the words to one of his disciples who was able to write and who inscribed them on the shoulder blades of sheep. Thus in time the Koran, the Holy Word

of God of the Mussulmans, appeared. The special prophets of God, according to the Koran, are Adam, Noah,
Abraham, Moses, Jesus, and Mahomet, each rising, in the
order named, superior to the other; Mahomet being the
greatest.

The seal of divine inspiration that is placed upon the
Koran outranks by far all the decisions pronounced upon
the New Testament by the bishops at Constantine's Council of Nice. We are told that the angel Gabriel brought to
Mahomet the identical volume of Scriptures, bound in silk
and precious stones, that was used in heaven, and which
was the personal property of God himself.

No canon law can come anywhere near competing with
this claim.

As to the miracles performed by Mahomet to prove
that he was chosen of God, accounts of which began to
be religiously circulated a few years after his death, they
even outclass those told of Christ. No wonder—Mahomet, claim the Mussulmans, was the Holy Ghost himself. Says Gibbon: "The evangelic promise of the *Para-
clete,* or Holy Ghost, was prefigured in the name and accomplished in the person, of Mahomet, the greatest and
last of the apostles of God." By a jugglery of the
"prophecies" contained in the Scriptures concerning the
manifestation of the Holy Ghost, and a few changes of
the Greek letters that spell the Ghost's name, the Mussulmans have shown that the etymology of the name Mahomet fulfills the prophecies. Theologians are adepts at
this sort of work. If, therefore, the Christian claim of
Jesus having been begotten by the Holy Ghost were true,

then the Mussulman claim would make Mahomet Jesus' father. And the faith that proves the one just as readily proves the other.

The parentage of Mahomet, while boasting no immaculate conceptions, was marked by a marvelous manifestation. He was the only son of Abdallah, who, we are told, "was the most beautiful and modest of the Arabian youth," and Amina, a beautiful Jewess, and of the noble race of the Zahrites. On the night of Abdallah's marriage to Amina, say the Mussulmans, "two hundred virgins expired of jealousy and despair."

No such inconsolable exhibition of grief and disappointment at not becoming mother of a god occurred when the Holy Ghost picked out the Virgin Mary.

Among the many miracles and wonders told of Mahomet it is recorded that trees walked forth to meet him; stones would rise up in the air and salute him; when, while traveling in the desert, he became thirsty, cold water gushed from his fingers; he fed the hungry by the miraculous creation of food, healed the sick and raised the dead to life; a camel, upon approaching Mahomet, was given the power of speech and talked to the prophet; also a dove from Paradise would fly down and perch on his shoulder and whisper in his ear; an enemy at one time poisoned a shoulder of mutton that was prepared for Mahomet's meal; the shoulder of mutton turned over in the dish and informed Mahomet of what had been done to it. The angel Gabriel was a constant companion of Mahomet's, and the two took frequent journeys together to Paradise to consult with God. Mahomet was furnished with a mysterious animal, called the Borak, that was bred in Paradise, upon whose back he made nightly trips from Mecca to Jerusalem and back. We are told that "with his companion, Gabriel, he successively ascended the seven heavens, and received and repaid the salutations of the patriarchs, the prophets, and the angels, in their respective mansions. Beyond the seventh heaven, Mahomet alone was permitted to proceed; he passed the veil of unity, approached within two bow-shots of the throne, and felt a cold wave that pierced him to the heart, when his shoulder was touched by the hand of God." After this familiar visit with God he again "descended to Jerusalem, remounted the Borak, returned to Mecca, and performed in the tenth part of a night the journey of many thousand years."

The first heaven, we are told, was of solid silver. There Mahomet met Adam, who embraced him, and gave thanks to God for having at last given him a son who could save the world. There also Mahomet gazed with wonder at the countless golden chains that hung from the silver foundation, and at the ends of which the stars were fastened.

Mahomet and Moses, it will be noted, both taught the same school of astronomy.

The second heaven was of solid gold, and there Mahomet met Noah. The third heaven was composed of precious stones. Upon his arriving there the first person that Mahomet recognized was Abraham. The two, however, had barely shaken hands, when Mahomet was startled by the appearance of an angel of most stupendous dimensions. To give an idea of the size of this angel, we are informed that the distance between his eyes was "seventy thousand days' journey," and his height was "five million and forty thousand days' journey."

A Mussulman has to have as much faith as a Christian in order to get to heaven.

The fourth heaven was of emerald. Joseph, the son of Jacob, was in charge of this heaven, and welcomed Mahomet. The fifth heaven was built of adamant. This was the residence of Moses. The sixth heaven was of solid carbuncle, and was the home of John the Baptist. The seventh heaven Mahomet found to be the end of the universe, constructed of all manner of brilliant jewels. Unlike the other heavens, there was no apartment overhead. It was the top flat. Beyond it was empty space, filled with flocks of flying angels accompanied by houris of dazzling beauty. Wonderful and strange creatures were some of these angels. One of them is described as having seventy thousand heads, with seventy thousand mouths that sang seventy thousand different songs at once to the glory of God. Christ was the general overseer and manager of this heaven. He held the job until Mahomet superseded him. And here, upon an elevated throne of pure gold, God himself sat and by his magic governed and controlled all creation. His splendor and size was beyond the uttermost limits of human imagination. Mahomet, as told, could only approach within two bow-shots of him. Mahomet could not have endured to have stood even this close if Jehovah had not covered his face with seventy thousand veils.

Mahomet's description of Paradise is thus seen to be much more clear and definite than that of the inspired author of the Book of Revelations.

At one time Mahomet was delivering a sermon at Mecca, and, so great was his oratory, and so powerful his voice, that he "split asunder the orb of the moon, and the obedient planet stooped from her station in the sky, accomplished the seven revolutions round the Caaba, saluted Mahomet in the Arabian tongue, and, suddenly contracting her dimensions, entered at the collar, and issued forth through the sleeve of his shirt."

Mahomet was a most faithful follower of the God Jehovah. He believed in human slavery; he believed in polygamy, and taught and practiced it; in fact, he believed in the Scriptures. He started out to convert the world in true Biblical style—by force of arms. He handled the "infidels" as Jehovah did the Midianites. With the sword the Mussulmans carried the faith into western Asia and all of northern Africa, and into Spain. They captured Jerusalem, and guarded the alleged sepulchre of Christ. For years the Christians and the Mussulmans fought for supremacy, each hating and cursing the other. Finally the Christians, under Charles the Hammer, on the field of Tours, overwhelmingly defeated the Moslems, slaying, so it is claimed, over three hundred thousand of the enemy. "But for this," writes Gibbon, "perhaps the interpretation of the Koran would now be taught in the schools of Oxford, and her pulpit would demonstrate to a circumcised people the sanctity and truth of the revelation of Mahomet."

Which creed—that of Constantine or that of Mahomet —would have been the worse, is hard to decide. Both bind in slavery the body and brain. Nor could the Crescent lead to bloodier slaughter than the Cross has led. No king or kaiser or czar of Europe, or capitalist ruler of America, though he knelt in prayer to Allah at daybreak, noon and evening, with eyes turned toward Mecca, could outrage the race more than the powers that be, that follow the creed of Constantine, have done.

The creed of Constantine, with its trinity of gods and hosts of saints, its rites and ceremonies, its immaculate conceptions, its incense and altars, and "virgin" priests and nuns, all copied after the ancient Roman mythology, naturally appealed to a people reared under paganism; while the religion of Mahomet found its most fertile soil where Judaism had implanted the belief in one God. Besides, wherever Judaism went, there polygamy was sanctioned. Monogamy is an inheritance from ancient Rome, and was originally established, not as a virtue, nor as a part of religious belief, but as an economic measure to prevent the patricians from appropriating so many of the healthiest and handsomest of the women that not enough were left for the plebians to reproduce a sufficient number of their species to supply the labor market.

Let us for a moment review and analyze the claims of the creed of Constantine. Let us take a look at its supernatural and spectacular origin, its sorceries and sensations, its marvelous and miraculous exhibitions, its final and eternal promises and threats. As the world's most insane "inspiration" it is well worth dragging into the limelight and looking over.

A little over nineteen hundred years ago the God Jehovah, who sits in splendor upon a gold throne millions of miles up in the skies, and to whom for centuries beasts and human beings have been offered in sacrifice by his chosen people to appease his awful wrath, left his celestial abode and located in Judea. There he could be seen hanging around the humble home of a beautiful maiden by the name of Mary, who was engaged to be married to a Jewish carpenter named Joseph. We know she was beautiful, because a divinely inspired oracle, St. Danniani, says that "God himself, on account of the surpassing beauty of the holy virgin, fell desperately in love with her;" and we know that the God Jehovah must have been recognized, because no creature of his size and general appearance could possibly hide or disguise himself. Here is his description, as witnessed by the divinely inspired saint that saw him on the Island of Patmos:

"And there sat in the midst of the seven golden candlesticks one like the Son of man, clothed with a garment down to the foot, and girt about the paps with a golden girdle. His head and his hairs were white like wool, as white as snow; and his eyes were as a flame of fire; and his feet like unto fine brass, as if they burned in a furnace; and his voice as the sound of many waters. And he had on his right hand seven stars; and out of his mouth went a sharp, two-edged sword; and his countenance was as the sun shineth in his strength."

He was like the "son of man"—that is, he was an anthropoidal god, built like a human, only bigger.

As a similar description is given in the eighteenth chapter of Psalms, verse 8, and also in the third chapter of Habakkuk, verse 4, we know there can be no mistake about it. Moses, we are told in the thirty-third chapter of Exodus, verse 23, once got a glimpse of his hind parts and it nearly blinded him. No—when Jehovah was spooning with Mary it is inconceivable to think that he went about incognito. It must have been known that he was in town, even if the natives did not realize at the time what he was up to.

Finally, even as often happens among frail mortals, Jehovah accomplished his designs, and the charming Mary found herself in a delicate condition. This might have upset Joseph, had not Jehovah, who, so it appears, had deserted the girl, sent an angel to Bethlehem, who hunted up Joseph's carpenter shop, and finally convinced him that he was going to become the stepfather of a young god.

The sight of an angel flying through the air from heaven to earth and back again was not uncommon in those days, so the people thought nothing about it. In fact, when Jehovah's and Mary's baby was born, it is claimed that flocks of angels, playing harps and singing songs, and announcing through trumpets the birth of a new god, were seen and heard throughout the country for miles around Bethlehem.

Such was the supernatural and spectacular origin of the Christian religion.

When the son of the God Jehovah grew to manhood he demonstrated his divinity by overturning all the laws of nature, from changing water into wine to raising the dead. He performed all manner of jugglery daily in public, and the Jews, strange to relate, seemed to take it all as a joke. A god was among them who could spit on the eyes of a blind man and restore his sight, or drive devils out of lunatics and herd them into droves of hogs, and yet the people repudiated him.

They couldn't help it—Jehovah had hardened their hearts and blinded their eyes.

Otherwise the Jews would not have carried out the premeditated purpose for which Jehovah had seduced Mary of Bethlehem.

And therein lies the marvelous mystery of the whole Christian creed. In order to comprehend it, you have to renounce your reason and go it by faith. The ancestress of the whole human race, who was created from a bone, ate an apple from a tree which Jehovah had forbidden her to touch, because, in spite of Jehovah's warning, a snake had advised her to do so. This brought Jehovah's curse upon her and all her posterity. The only thing that appeared to partially appease Jehovah's wrath was the smell of the blood of animal and human sacrifices; and finally this became stale to his nostrils. (See the Life of Jehovah, Chapter VI, in regard to human sacrifices having been offered to Jehovah.) Something extraordinary, said Jehovah, had to be done in order to stop him from everlastingly damning the entire human race.

He thought he ought to save a few of them.

So he, the alleged creator of all the universe, conceived the "Christian plan of salvation"—the bloody sacrifice of a god. He successfully worked out his scheme, the people sacrificed his son Jesus, and if you believe all this your sins will be washed away in Jesus' blood. If not, you go to eternal torment.

The canonization of the books of the Bible, done by Constantine's bishops at the Council of Nice, that declares these books to be "divinely inspired," is the charm that for centuries has held the common people in superstitious submission to the plundering powers that be.

"The powers that be are ordained of God"—therefore "be ye subject unto them." The Masters and the God are partners. They own you. You dare not think differently than the Book that the God wrote. You dare not act differently than the Laws that the Masters make. You are of one class—they of another. It is yours to toil—it is theirs to take; yours to fast, theirs to feast; yours to wear rags, theirs to adorn themselves in robes. You have no home, no country. They own the earth. You are a renter—they are the rulers. They are rich by the ruin of you. You work for them and fight for them, live for them and die for them. They are ordained by their God, and you are damned by the same God if you dare to doubt or rebel.

Regardless of their threatened hell hereafter, the Christian creed has put you in a hell of a fix here.

True, these class distinctions—this society of masters and slaves—exist in countries where Christianity is unknown, and existed before the Christian creed was constructed; but of all the world's great religions, Christianity is the only one that carries a club of "believe or be damned" in its clutches. The Christian God is the only myth that runs an eternal torment resort for those who dare to do their own thinking; and the Christian war-lords, aping this myth, have done their best to make this earth look like their fabled hell.

The followers of Buddha, who far outnumber the followers of Constantine, do not stain the earth with rivers of blood in mad war. They have no example to follow of a God butchering Midianite men, women and children, and turning the maidens over to be raped by Jehovah's soldiers. Buddha did not reveal any such monster, and his four-hundred and fifty millions of followers do not fear him. Listen to the words of Buddha, and compare them to the promises and threats with which the New Testament abounds:

"I do not care to know your various theories about God. What is the use of discussing all the subtle doctrines about the soul? Do good and be good. And this will take you to whatever truth there is."

"Believe not because some old manuscripts are produced, believe not because it is your national belief, because you have been made to believe from your childhood, but reason truth out, and after you have analyzed it, then, if you find it will do good to one and all, believe it, live up to it, and help others to live up to it."

These are the words of Buddha.

The Christians that have made a human slaughterhouse of the world send missionaries to convert his followers to the glad tidings of eternal torment to all heathen and heretics.

Compare the words of Buddha, that to "do good and be good will take you to whatever truth there is," to the Christian creed of a vicarious atonement—the loading of your sins on Jesus—the washing away of your crimes in the blood of a sacrificed deity!

I do not for a moment think that the man Jesus—the carpenter—ever dreamed that years after his death pagan priests would transform him into a sacrificed offering to a barbaric god. I believe that the religion of Jesus was probably much like the religion of Buddha, that he was born of the proletariat class, and that he was put to death as a dangerous revolter against the Roman master class. I believe there is enough evidence to prove that he taught a simple gospel of human brotherhood, peace and love. I believe that if Jesus were here he would be the first to expose the impostors that have turned his message into a fraud and fable in the interests of the very masters of bread and Pharisees that he fearlessly denounced and defied.

Neither do I assert that all the writings found in the Bible are barbarous. Some of the old Hebrew prophets —meaning teachers—were splendid men, voicing the highest hopes and aspirations of the race. They, too, were made martyrs to the cause of human freedom. Isaiah, denouncing the religion of sacrifices and burnt offerings, visioned, not the savage Jehovah, but the Spirit of love and justice, whom he makes to declare, "I delight not in the blood of bullocks, or of lambs, or of he goats. * * * Learn to do well; seek justice, relieve the oppressed, help the fatherless, plead for the widow."

Isaiah was condemned by the priests and rulers of his day as a rebellious heretic, and was sawed asunder in a hollow tree. His religion was the religion of humanity. After him came the greatest of the Hebrew teachers, the Great Unknown, whose writings are found in the fortieth to the sixty-sixth chapters of the Book of Isaiah. These, as acknowledged by both Jewish and Gentile scholars, were added after Isaiah's death.

Such splendid souls do not belong to the believe-or-be-damned Christians. They belong to oppressed and out-raged and robbed Humanity. They have nothing in common with exploiters and war wolves. Their voices still call in revolt against the creed of Constantine.

Listen to the true story of the race, as revealed by modern science:

The first habitable earth was a swamp, the home of our ancestors the reptiles. The ancestors of the reptiles were the denizens of the deep, from whence originated all life. The creation of man did not start with a cultured gentleman and lady, carrying a prayerbook in their hands, and dwelling in a luxurious garden. It began with creeping creatures and lizards that dwelt on a bog. These evolved into monsters with necks long enough to enable them to feed on the leaves of the huge, tropical trees. It required hundreds of thousands of years to evolve the first anthropoid apes, one branch of which family, through the law of natural selection, at last became the direct progenitors of the human race. In civilized man courses the blood of the lowest fishes, the amphibian, reptilian and mammalian species. This is also true of all mammals.

We all carry to this day the birthmarks of this common ancestry. A chick of three to five days' incubation, has four gill-slits on the side of the neck. In human embryos of three to five weeks' development appear these gill-slits. All reptiles, birds and mammals possess them. These gill-slits serve no function with purely air-breathing creatures, and close long before hatching or birth. They only serve as a biologic evidence of our remote ancestors of the sea.

In the early embryos of all higher forms of life is found the notachord, the dorsal stiffening axis of the lower vertebrates. This disappears as the backbone develops.

In man, and in all other mammals, three distinct pairs of kidneys appear in the early embryonic stage. The first kidneys develop at the stage when the fish-gills are formed, and are identical with the kidneys of the lowest species of fishes. The second kidneys appear at the amphibian-reptilian stage of embryonic life, and with the amphibia, such as frogs, crocodiles, beavers and such like creatures as can live in both air and water, persist throughout life. The third kidneys succeed these in the development of mammals, and remain, whilst the other two, and useless ones, perish.

Thus again has Nature preserved the story of our origin.

Abundance of other similar evidence of our common ancestry exists, that can be found in any standard work on biology.

The science of comparative embryology stands an irrefutable witness to Darwin's theory of the descent of man. Says Le Conte: "By the law of heredity each generation repeats the form and structure of the previous, and in the order in which they successively appeared. But there is a tendency for each successively appearing character to appear a little earlier in each successive generation; and by this means time is left over for the introduction of still higher new characters. Thus, characters which were once adult are pushed back to the young, and then still back to the embryo, and thus place and time are made for each generation to push on still higher."

A wonderful story has Nature imperishably inscribed in our bodies, telling of our origin and progress through the ever evolving ages! A story rich in knowledge and infinite hope for the future!

Well may we feel assured, as we trace our journey from the jungle world, that the resistless laws of Evolution and the Survival of the Fittest will at last people the world with a Humanity that has triumphed over the beast, that has discarded the fang and claw!

CHAPTER III

THE purpose of the creed of Constantine, viz: to hold the masses in superstitious servility, is disclosed, when analyzed, in the fabulous lives of the saints, which became part of the faith the church imposed upon believers. These saints rapidly took the places of the discarded pagan gods and goddesses, and are worshiped by the faithful of the Roman church. That the Protestants denounce the worship of these saints, and confine their adoration to the Holy Trinity, does not alter the fact that the lesson contained in the stories told of the saints is the backbone of the Protestant faith.

Humility, submission, contentment with your lot— these be the very essence of orthodox Christianity.

Among the divinest of the saints stands St. Joseph, the alleged foster-father of God. He ranks next to the Virgin Mary, the mother of God. St. Joseph, according to the Roman Church, is the holiest human male that ever lived. A minute biography of this saint, "taken," we are told, "from the Mystical City of God," is "The Admirable Life of the Glorious Patriarch Saint Joseph," written by the Abbe Boullan. This work has the approbation of the Holy See, and therefore is "divinely inspired." "Read the book," declares the reverend author. "and study it without hesitation; for Rome, who cannot err, has spoken."

The life of this saint and pillar upon which the creed of Constantine rests, as told by the Abbe Boullan, is surely interesting. It is instructive and amusing. It is a credit to the priesthood that originated the gods of mythology. After paying due respect to the Virgin Mary, who, we are informed, had taken the vow of life-long chastity and was living as a nun in the Temple at Jerusalem, the author proceeds to describe the wedding of the Holy Virgin—whom the Roman Church declares to have been, like Jesus, divinely conceived—to Saint Joseph, who also had taken the vow of life-long chastity.

The object for such a marriage as this, like the riddle of the three gods in one, can only be explained by the mysteries of theology.

The divinely inspired report of this remarkable wedding, as found in the work of the Abbe Boullan, runs as follows:

"The Lord spoke in a dream to the high-priest, who was St. Simeon, and commanded him to make preparations for the marriage of Mary, daughter of Joachim and Anne of Nazareth, and to convoke an assemblage of the other priests to deliberate upon the subject. St. Simeon obeyed the divine behest, and the assembled doctors, inspired by a celestial impulse, resolved, that in an affair upon which the Lord had declared His good pleasure, they ought to consult His holy will by praying, that He would manifest, by a sign, him who should be the husband of Mary, and that he should be of the house and lineage of David, that the law might be fulfilled. They therefore resolved to appoint a day when all the young men of that family, present in Jerusalem, should be invited to assemble in the Temple. It was precisely the day on which our Blessed Lady had attained her fourteenth year."

Those acquainted with the Old Testament account of King David's domestic affairs will readily admit that, in the ordinary nature of things, the woods around Jerusalem were likely to have been full of his royal progeny.

The story proceeds:

"The Priest Simeon summoned the chaste Mary, in order to make known to her this resolution. It was nine days before that on which their designs were to be put into execution. During this time the most Blessed Virgin redoubled her prayers, her tears, and sighs, for the accomplishment of the will of God in an event which caused her the greatest pain."

Mary, realizing what the God Jehovah purposed regarding her, apparently did not relish the proposition of being united in marriage to a creature of flesh and blood. That she was doubtless aware of the part she was destined to play in theological circles is disclosed in the "Life of the Blessed Virgin Mary, Mother of God," by the Abbi Orsini, another work that is recognized by Rome as authoritative. In this work we are informed that the Holy Virgin, while an inmate of the Temple, was said to have frequented the "HOLY OF HOLIES," the private apartment occupied by Jehovah himself. She was the only female, so we are told, that ever passed the threshold of this mysterious chamber, of which the following description is given: "The HOLY OF HOLIES, that impenetrable sanctuary of the God of Hosts, was closed to the whole Hebrew priesthood except the high-priest, who entered it but once a year, after much fasting, watching, and purification. He only presented himself there in the midst of a thick cloud of incense, which interposed between him and the Divinity, whom no man can see and live, says the Scriptures. Finally, he remained there but a few minutes, while the people, prostrate on the ground, sobbed and wept, fearing he should meet his death. He himself afterwards gave a grand banquet to his friends, to rejoice with them for having escaped such imminent and fearful danger."

If the Virgin Mary had access to this mysterious and fearful private apartment, where the God Jehovah sat alone in fire and fury, she must have been put next to all that was about to happen to her. No wonder then that the thought of her marriage to a human being "caused her the greatest pain." It was enough to drive her crazy.

But "the Lord consoled her," writes the inspired Abbe Boullan, saying, " 'I will give you a spouse who will not oppose your holy desires, but who will rather, by the help of my grace, confirm them. I will choose him for you perfect, and according to my own heart, and I will elect him for you from among my servants.' The holy angels also consoled her, saying: 'The Most High will guide you in the way which is best, the most perfect, the most holy.'"

"The day appointed by the priests," continues the narrative, "arrived. Our Blessed Lady had completed the fourteenth year of her age. The young men of the tribe of Judah, and of the family of David, from whom the august Mary was descended, who were in the city of Jerusalem, were assembled."

(The reader will note that nothing but the "royal blood" of the master-class would do to start the creed of Constantine.)

The account goes on: "Joseph, originally of Nazareth, but now an inhabitant of the holy city, was invited to be with them, because he, too, was of that royal race. He was then thirty-three years of age, well-made, and possessed of an agreeable physiognomy, which expressed an incomparable modesty."

According to this Roman Catholic authority, endorsed by the Holy See, St. Joseph remained pure and spotless all his life. The Abbe Boullan contradicts the New Testament account that says that Jesus had a number of brothers (Matthew XIII, verse 55). This, however, should not worry the faithful, as the inspired Scriptures are full of contradictions.

"He (St. Joseph)," continues the Abbe Boullan, "was indeed as chaste in his thoughts and deeds, as in his inclinations; and having made a vow of chastity when but twelve years old, his life was pure and irreproachable before God and man. He was related to the Virgin Mary in the third degree.

"Inspired by the Most High, the chief-priest placed in the hands of each of these young men a dry rod, in order that by this means the Lord should manifest him whom He had chosen to be the husband of Mary. All united their prayers to those of the priests, for none were ignorant of the virtues and modesty of this holy maiden, nor of the reputation of her beauty, and her possessions, as an only child; and each desired to make her his wife. Joseph alone, the most humble, the most pious among them, deemed himself unworthy of so great a boon; and, calling to mind his vow of chastity, he resolved anew to observe it, resigning himself to the divine will even to the end of his life."

It was certainly a most trying ordeal that the chosen groom of the young and beautiful Mary was called to pass through. That is, if he was in good health.

The tale proceeds: "All were engaged in prayer, when they saw blossoms burst forth from the rod borne by Joseph, which alighted at the head of the saint. The Lord, at the same moment, spoke to him interiorly, and said: 'Joseph, my servant, Mary shall become your spouse; receive her with assiduity and respect, for she is very agreeable in my eyes.' "

Then, we are told, "the priests, upon this sign from heaven, determined to give St. Joseph to Mary for her husband."

An account of Mary's surpassing beauty follows: "They then called for her, who was more excellent than the sun, more beautiful than the moon, and she appeared with a majesty more than angelic; with a loveliness, modesty, and grace incomparable."

And so were St. Joseph and the Virgin Mary united in a mock-marriage, and started on a mock-honeymoon to the saint's humble home in Nazareth. Mary, who was now called Queen of the Universe, was, we are informed, attended by a thousand angels. Evidently Jehovah thought, notwithstanding St. Joseph's vows, that it might be a little risky to trust her alone with him.

The Jews have left no record of all these wonders taking place around their Temple. It remained for Roman priests, years afterwards, to tell us of them through divine inspiration. Otherwise the story of St. Joseph and the Virgin Mary would have been lost to the world.

That there might be no misunderstanding from the start regarding the conditions that Jehovah had imposed upon St. Joseph and his bride, the following conversation, upon their arrival at St. Joseph's home, is reported to have occurred between the pair; said the Virgin Mary to St. Joseph: "It is just that we offer thanks, and give glory and praise to our God and Creator, who has made His mercy to shine upon us, in choosing us for His service. In my most tender youth, I consecrated myself to God by a vow which I made, to be, during all my life, chaste in body and mind, and my desire to preserve my faith in Him is unchangeable. I trust that you will help me to fulfill this vow, and in all things else I will be your servant. Accept, my husband, this holy resolution, and confirm it by your own, so that we may obtain the eternal joys for which we aspire."

These remarks, we are told, pleased her husband, he being a saint.

"The chaste Joseph," records the Abbe Boullan, "filled with joy, replied: 'In declaring to me your chaste thoughts and holy resolutions, you have penetrated and opened my heart, which, until you had revealed your own, I was unwilling to uncover. The Lord called me, also, at an early age, that I should love Him with an upright mind. Know, then, that in my twelfth year I, too, made a promise to serve God in perpetual chastity. I now renew this vow, and, with His grace, I will be your faithful servant, and I pray you to receive my chaste affections, and to regard me as your brother.' "

A worthy beginning for a creed that "made birth a sin, life a nightmare and death a horror!"

We are told that "during this conversation the Most High confirmed anew in the heart of St. Joseph the virtue of chastity, and the pure and holy love which he should bear to the Blessed Virgin, his spouse. Thus he was possessed by this love in an eminent degree, and our august Queen augmented it, and enraptured his heart by her conversation. By this divine assistance the holy spouses enjoyed inexpressible consolation. The august Queen promised to second the desires of St. Joseph, and the Most High imbued him with such an exalted purity, and such an absolute control of his passions, that he served his consort without obstacle, and with a grace as admirable as it was extraordinary."

St. Joseph never kissed his charming bride. He never put his arm around her waist, or squeezed her dainty hand.

And the church, backed by the New Testament, tells us that such is "holiness" and the "will of God," and "following in Christ's footsteps."

And the doctors tells us that it has filled the world with insanity.

So far as can be ascertained from the Abbe Boullan's biography, St. Joseph was never alone with the beautiful Mary for a single instant. She occupied a room by herself, in which she was chaperoned at all hours of the day and night by a company of able-bodied male angels. St. Joseph used to visit the Virgin's private apartment, and would sit and talk to the angels. Says the inspired Abbe Boullan: "St. Joseph never saw his holy spouse asleep. He did not know, from his own experience, whether she slept at all."

There can, therefore, be no doubt, if the record be trustworthy, but that St. Joseph was a real saint.

He, together with his virgin bride, we are told, lived in abject poverty and humility. Probably, like the saints of a later period, he went through life without ever taking a bath.

When a little past middle age he became a physical wreck. Following the life of a saint may have been fine for his soul, but seems to have been hard on his health. Soon after the Virgin's son of God was born St. Joseph became so weak that he could not do a day's work. He was of no account whatever except for fast-

ing and praying.   Jehovah's angels could have safely
gone back to heaven, and left the poor old worn-out
saint alone with Mary.

The poverty of the holy couple became so intense that
Mary had to take in washing, or perform some other
like womanly occupation, to support the family, for, says
the Abbe Boullan, "The Blessed Virgin charged herself
with the support of her most holy Son and her spouse,
by her work."

And the inspired writer draws from this a message to
the world's poverty-stricken masses.   He says: "The
Lord offers this strong woman to us as an example."

To be sure he does.

"Let the women do the work."

In fact, the entire fable of St. Joseph, the Holy Virgin, and the incarnate son of the God Jehovah, is a most
admirable myth to make the exploited masses contented
with their earthly lot.   The Abbe Boullan informs us
that just prior to the birth of Jehovah's son, St. Joseph
and the Holy Virgin knelt in prayer, and that "while
they were engaged in prayer, the Most High replied to
each in particular by the same voice: 'I have descended
from heaven to earth to elevate humility, and to debase
pride—to honor poverty, and to make riches contemptible.'"   This was Jesus speaking from his mother's
womb.   He did this quite frequently during the months
before he was born, according to the Catholic authority
quoted.

"To honor poverty!"   Alas! for nearly two thousand
years have the world's toilers received this on bended

knees, from pious plunderers reveling in "contemptible" riches!

Occasionally, we are told, when starvation actually stared the Holy Family in the face, angels from heaven brought them food. This is told to show the church's approval of charity. "Let the poor rejoice in this example," says the author of the Life of St. Joseph; "let not the hungry be cast down—let those who suffer persecution expect help in season, and let none complain of divine Providence!"

Socialism, that would allow you to feed yourself, instead of being dependent upon "divine Providence," is wicked in the sight of the creed of Constantine.

At one time St. Joseph, being too infirm to work, and the Holy Virgin being unable to find any, and the angels evidently too busy singing hallelujahs to hurry to earth with a handout, the infant son of the God Jehovah was about to perish with hunger; so St. Joseph, as a last resort, went around to the back doors in the neighborhood and begged some food. "By this example," we are told, "he teaches the poor never to complain of their wants, nor to be ashamed to beg, when all other legitimate means have failed, since it was necessary to beg at so early a period to support the life of the Lord of all created things."

This is the accepted doctrine of the church. To deny it, when the church was in full power, meant the rack and torture, and the burning alive at the stake; for to destroy the injunctions of humility and obedience to the master-class, of contentment in poverty and rags, de-

stroys the very intent and foundation upon which orthodox Christianity is built.

The evidence offered by Roman Catholic authorities
to prove the story of the divine conception of Jesus, as
well as that of the divine conception of his mother, is
somewhat remarkable. They present the legends of
heathen gods and goddesses, and virgin mothers of
heathen divinities, thereby virtually claiming that these
legends are all true.

The ancient world was overrun with divinely begotten
gods and saviors.

The Protestant theologians denounce all these heathen
divinities. They repudiate them as myths, and claim that
their own myths, taken bodily from the Roman Church,
are the only true myths. The Protestants disdain to
offer any sort of evidence. They have none. They walk
by faith alone.

"Let us survey the various regions of the globe,"
writes the Abbe Orsini, in his "Life of the Blessed Virgin
Mary, Mother of God." "Let us search, from north to
south, from east to west, the religious chronicles of the
nations, we shall find the Virgin promised at the basis
of almost all theogonies."

Theogony, as the reader will note by referring to any
standard dictionary, means the generation of the heathen
gods; while theology means the generation of the Christian gods. A slight difference in spelling is all that sep-
arates the one from the other.

And then the Abbe Orsini, in order to show that the
Roman Catholic story of the Virgin Mary and her

divinely conceived offspring is nothing out of the ordinary in religious happenings—in fact, has a large number of precedents—recounts the appearance, at different periods and divers places, of gods born of virgins. He recalls the story of the god Fo, of Thibet, who had himself conceived in the womb of a young and beautiful fairy, named Lhamoghiuprul, who was betrothed to the king; of the Emperor of China, Hoang-Ti, a son of heaven, whose mother conceived by a flash of lightning; of another Chinese emperor, Yao, born of a virgin who conceived one night from the beam of a star shining in her bed-chamber; of Yu, the head of the first Chinese dynasty, who came into this world by the power of a pearl that a Chinese god flung from heaven, and which landed in the bosom of a Chinese virgin; of Heou-Tsi, of the dynasty of Tcheou, whose virgin mother became pregnant by saying her prayers. The account of the miraculous births of these divinely ordained rulers, argues the Roman Catholic authority quoted, "renders the resemblance to the divine maternity of Mary still more striking."

To be sure it does. From a theological standpoint it is all the evidence necessary. Many of the ancient rulers of earth, including Alexander of Macedon, claimed divine origin. They or their ancestors were begotten of a god. Tyrants assumed divinity in order to overawe their exploited subjects. And the creed of the Emperor Constantine, for the same purpose, made a divinely conceived royal divinity of the lowly Jesus. "King by the grace of God" is but the echo of the ancient boast of these royal robbers, "King by divine birth."

All the races of earth have been despoiled by "divinely begotten" despots and saviors, upheld by "divinely inspired" creeds. The Druids were expecting their god Esus, to whom they offered maidens in sacrifice, to beget a god, when along came the Christians with one already begotten. This satisfied the Druids, and they accepted Christianity. This is another proof of the truth of Christianity.

In accepting, with the approval of Rome, all the virgin births of deities he could find among the legends of Asia, the Abbe Orsini exclaims: "No, it is not by chance that the mystery of the incarnation of a God in the womb of a virgin is one of the fundamental doctrines of Asia. It is not by chance that the privileged women who bear in their womb that emanation of the Divinity are always chaste, beautiful and holy."

The gods have always not only chosen as mates the chaste and holy, but also the most charming of the daughters of men.

The divinely inspired Abbe Orsini, like the divinely inspired apocryphal Gospel of the Nativity of Mary, differs with the divinely inspired Abbe Boullan regarding the age and health of St. Joseph at the time of his marriage to the mother of God. The Abbe Orsini declares that the earthly husband of the Virgin was "a man of advanced age, a decayed patrician," and that it was on account of his infirmities that he was selected by the holy priests.

Considering the neutral part that this saint was destined to play in the divine comedy the "advanced age" and "decayed" story does seem the more reasonable.

The faithful, however, should have no difficulty in accepting both accounts.

The beautiful Mary, we are told, had many admirers who were neither old nor decayed. One of these, says the Roman Catholic "History of Carmel," named Agabus, "a young and wealthy patrician," became brokenhearted at the sight of Mary's marriage to the decrepit and decayed Joseph, and renounced his riches and went and dwelt in a cave. After the birth of Christ he became a Christian monk, and thereby saved his soul. Thus does Jehovah reward the faithful.

In prostituting the simple message of human brotherhood and peace into a religion to suit the ruling classes, the priests of the creed of Constantine have experienced considerable difficulty in removing the odium, in the eyes of the powers that be, as found in the early account of Jesus' lowly origin. The Abbe Orsini, in order to awe the masses and tickle the ears of princes, says: "Now, Joseph, although poor, was of the Davidical race. The blood of twenty kings flowed in his veins. * * * The holy daughter of Joachim did not lower herself, therefore, as much as might be thought by espousing the carpenter." Mary, be it remembered, was, according to the church, also of royal blood. Christ was therefore, according to the creed of Constantine, not only of divine heavenly blood, but also of royal earthly blood. He would be eligible to marry into the royal families were he living today. It was only on account of financial reverses that St. Joseph was compelled to earn his living shingling roofs. It was unfortunate, and is to be regretted, but at the time Joseph was the only live saint that was far enough along in years and sufficiently decayed to answer Jehovah's purpose, so after all, "the holy daughter of Joachim did not lower herself as much as might be thought."

With this apology for the seeming low class of society into which Christ was born, the holy fathers have made their creed acceptable to the world's aristocrats.

The wedding of Joseph and Mary was a swell affair, according to the Abbe Orsini. He thus describes it: "It was a bright winter's day, and the new moon was slowly rising behind the mountains, when a long train of richly-dressed women was seen to approach the dwelling of Mary. The light of the torches, borne by a number of slaves, flashed on their cintures of gold, their strings of pearl, the jeweled crescents which they wore on their foreheads, and the diamonds of their Persian tiaras. Those daughters of Zion still retained the use of paint, which was known even in the days of Jezabel; their brows and eyelashes were painted black, and the tips of their fingers were red as the berries of the eglantine." We are told that they all belonged "to Jewish society." Mary herself was gorgeously arrayed, and to dispel any doubt of this, "there are," says the authority quoted, "two of the Virgin's tunics still preserved, and they are made of very precious stuff." Her robe is minutely described; "the ground was of a buff, or nankin color, interspersed with flowers of blue, white, violet and gold. It is now the holy relic of Chartres." We are informed that "numerous miracles have been attributed to it." Its preservation through all these years is another miracle. Into all this finery was brought the poor old, worn-out carpenter, Joseph. Doubtless, he was taken in charge by some well-to-do friend of the bride, his hickory shirt and overalls removed, and a proper dress suit loaned him for the occasion.

There is no account given of the whereabouts of Jehovah while all this was going on. It is strange the theologians have not placed him at the wedding feast, sitting on a gold throne behind a cloud of incense, with his blaze of fire blowing from his mouth and the smoke steaming from his nose (Psalms XVIII, verse 8), and the sharp horns on his fingers and the big sword in his mouth (Habakkuk, III, verse 4, and Revelations, I, verse 16). The wedding of the Virgin without Jehovah is like Hamlet with the ghost left out. He could have at least exposed his hind parts to the fashionable company, as he once did to Moses. Surely the originators of the Christian faith could not have considered it too much of a strain on the credulity of the masses to have pictured Jehovah's presence. Perhaps they merely overlooked the matter, and, if so, it should not be too late yet to rectify the oversight. It ought to be as easy to get a divine inspiration of the affair now as it was in the Dark Ages.

As far as can be ascertained, Jehovah did not exhibit himself until he had begotten himself, by the power of the Holy Ghost, who is also himself, in the womb of the Virgin Mary, in the person of his son, who is also himself, and who is also the Holy Ghost, and which all three are one, and all of which three in one are Jehovah.

It is not given to mortal man to unravel this. Even St. John of Chrysostom gave it up. "Let us dive no further," said he, "into this mystery."

In order to produce the mysterious doctrine of the Trinity, holy men of God went for days without anything to eat or drink; they put pebbles in the soles of their boots and bristles and briars under their shirts; they flagellated each other on their bare backs with whips of thorns; they lacerated their flesh with sharp stones; they slept on ash piles and never took a bath; and finally, under all this hungering and thirsting, blistering and scratching, flagellations and lacerations, sleepless nights and suffering days, they saw things. The doctrine of the Trinity is one of them.

But to return to Jehovah's first, and, as far as can be learned, last appearance, after the marriage of his mother, by himself, to Joseph. The Abbe Boullan, in the "Life of St. Joseph," thus describes it:

"St. Joseph meditated upon the Lord, whom the august Mary bore in her chaste bosom, adoring and rendering to Him honor and glory. Then, in recompense for his sanctity and his respect, mingled with fear, the Infant God, made man, sometimes manifested Himself in an admirable manner. He (Joseph) saw Him in the bosom of His most pure mother, as through a luminous crystal." Mary and Joseph would then pray to the unborn god, and the unborn god would audibly answer.

Nor should Protestants ridicule the "Life of the Blessed Virgin Mary" or the "Life of St. Joseph" as herein quoted, and as accepted by the Catholic Church. The Catholic Church is the source of all the faith that the Protestants possess, and the Abbe Orsini and the Abbe Boullan have just as much evidence of having been divinely inspired as has the author of the Book of Revelations, who saw a woman standing on the moon, with the sun wrapped about her body, and wearing a dozen stars for a bonnet (Revelations, XII, verse 1).

CHAPTER IV

SAYS James Anthony Froude, the English historian: "The endurance of the inequalities of life by the poor is the marvel of human society."

And it is.

The servility of one class of human beings to another class is the most astonishing thing in the history of the race. It would make wild animals wonder; it ought to make human beings blush for their breed.

It is something that deserves looking into. For there must be a reason for it. In all the universe there is no effect without a cause. And it seems strange that so great a scholar as James Anthony Froude did not realize this—or if he did, failed to find it. For it is not so hard to discover. All one needs to do is to look a slave over. It is easy enough to see what ails him. It is either power over the body, or power over the mind, or both. Nothing else would make him servile. It is a club or a creed. Or, more effective still, a club and a creed. In order to make him obedient, the slave must be made to fear.

In early society the master depended solely on the club. When the club failed to do the work, and the slave became rebellious, he was put to death. He was stoned by the worshipers of Jehovah and crucified by the worshipers of Jove. It was a financial loss to the master to kill him. It was like shooting a balky horse.

The slave was taught that he was a beast—that he had no soul. Only the masters had souls. They alone were of immortal birth. This was the teaching of Roman Mythology. When the priests of Mythology constructed this religion they were doing the best they knew how at that time to hold the masters in power and the slaves in servility. A religion that catalogued the slaves with barnyard cattle was a good one so long as the slaves accepted it. The priests of Mythology figured that if the slaves believed that this life was all there was for them, and that when they died that ended them, that they would then endure slavery rather than be killed— would submit to their beatings rather than rebel; for life is dear to all, and the spark of hope is hard to quench.

Then one day there appeared a bold rebel—"one of those damned agitators"—a carpenter by trade, who declared that the slaves had souls, that the race sprang from one common source, and that all blood is alike. This gospel of Love and Liberty and Fraternity and Immortality ran like riotous wine in the veins of the lowly. It flamed the spark of hope to raging fire. It made men of menials—men that dared death itself.

So the masters killed the carpenter—they hanged him on a cross as a rebel slave. But they did not kill his

message.   Others took it up, and they, too, were crucified, and burned, and fed to lions.   And still the message
would not die.   It was told in the dead of night, in
catacombs and caves, when the masters were sleeping
their drunken sleep.   And more were killed, and still
more; and the message thrived on martyrdom.   The
tomb lost its terrors when it became a doorway to immortality.

But alas! for the rebellious slaves and the message of
liberty.   A Pharisee came along and stabbed it.   He
wrote into the mouth of the carpenter a craven creed.
He commanded the slaves to be obedient to their masters, and subject unto the powers that be.   For the powers that be, said the Pharisee, are ordained of a god.
And he told the slaves not to look for happiness here,
but in a heaven beyond the stars.   And by and by the
priests of Mythology discovered in the teachings of the
Pharisee a better paregoric than their own religion con-.
tained.   So they wrote "gospels," full of promises and
threats, added them to the old scriptural slave laws, and
declared them all divinely inspired.   Obedient slaves
were assured an eternity spent in celestial mansions;
while the rebellious ones were doomed to everlasting torment.   With this superstition—this holy horror—pumped
into their brains by the priests, the masses of the people
became servile victims to the powers that be.

"The marvel of society," that James Anthony Froude
wondered at, becomes no marvel at all when society's
religious rags are torn off.   The fear of hell, as Robert
Burns told, "has held the wretch in order."   The creed

of Constantine has made a race of slaves—cringing cowards, frightened at the phantoms of priests, crawling on their knees to the plunderers that pick their pockets, willing to live and toil in poverty, or die fighting for their masters' glory.

When the African slaves were brought in shiploads to this country, the first thing their masters did was to teach them the Christian religion. It was all they were taught. It was considered as necessary as the overseer's lash. To teach a negro to read and write was a crime punishable by law. It was feared he might run across a grain of truth. Paul's epistles were all the "learning" allowed to enter his head.

Nor is Christianity the only religion purposed to hold the plundered poor in subjection. The world is full of such religions. The Chinese Joss and the Hindoo Brahma, the Mohammedan Allah and the Jewish Jehovah, these gods and many more are all largely patterned alike. They all ordain the powers that be to rule and rob the workers. This is fine for the rulers and robbers. Faith in phantoms is a positive preventative of knowledge and freedom. And no more servile slaves could be bred than those who faithfully follow the creed of Constantine, who postpone their happiness until after their funeral, and who believe to do otherwise means the everlasting torture of their souls. The masters that ordained the creed of Constantine only designed that the ignorant should accept it. It was not intended for the more enlightened. Pope Leo X expressed the sentiment of his class—"And all these privileges have been secured to us by the fable of Jesus Christ!"

Before the light of modern science these fables must flee; the priests that made them must soon hunt the asylums for recruits; in the twentieth century they will be gone.

We no longer hang a witch when epidemics sweep the land; we look to the board of health, these days, to find the filth that started the pest. Pulpits no longer thunder forth anathemas against comets; the astronomers, whom the priests used to burn alive, have told us what comets are, and we believe the astronomers rather than the priests. The dark nights no longer frighten the people with shadowy hydras and genii, ghosts and gorgons; electric lights have banished these. Women no longer are charged with sitting on a devil's cauldron and giving birth to sooterkins; when feeble-minded children are born now the doctors trace it to a syphilitic strain in one of the parents' or ancestors' blood. We are learning, slowly, but surely, that we are not in the hands of ghosts, and that the race itself is master of its own fate. Augury, and oracles, sorcery and divination are fading away; we are learning to turn to scholars, not saints, for knowledge. The delusions that have haunted human brains, that lit the fagots that burned thinkers, are being pushed back into the night whence they came.

Of the life and sayings of the man Jesus, comparatively little is known. It is the fabled Christ—the deified myth of Roman priestcraft—that the world is best acquainted with. There is, however, enough extant of the writings of the immediate followers of Jesus to disclose that his purpose and mission was not to establish a dogmatic religion, but to inaugurate a new dispensation—a society of equals in the means of life.

The religion of the fabled Christ has been a curse to mankind. It has held monsters on thrones and exploiters in power; it has made men murder each other to perpetuate their own bondage; and all because of the insane belief that it will save slaves that are subject to the powers that be, and send to hell all heretics and rebels. There isn't a war-demon that could hold his job if the people were not saturated with the superstition and servility of the creed of Constantine. The fabled Christ is the prize deity of the master-class. The infamy of it is that he is a mythical metamorphosis of a sweet-souled, lowly-born workingman that once dreamed a dream of a society of brothers, wherein there would be no masters, no poverty nor war.

The Jewish followers of Jesus were communists. The first Christian society was a workingclass revolt. For this they were beheaded, crucified, burned, and fed to wild beasts. Says Ernst Haeckel: "Primitive Christianity embraces the first three centuries. Christ himself the noble prophet and enthusiast, so full of the love of humanity, was far below the level of classical culture; he knew nothing beyond the Jewish traditions; he has not left a single linc of writing (Riddle of the Universe, page 311)." "The Christians of the early centuries were generally pure Communists, sometimes 'Social Democrats,' who, according to the prevailing theory in Germany today, ought to have been exterminated with fire and sword (ibid, page 314)."

The Sermon on the Mount—the only message the first followers of Jesus possessed—was preserved by word of mouth; Jesus did not leave a written line. That he and his disciples taught the equality of all mankind, communism and the immortality of the soul, is clearly evidenced by numerous writings of the period. Tertullian writes:

"Christians have no master and no Christian shall be bound for bread and raiment. The land is no man's inheritance; none shall possess it as property."

And Ambrose says:

"Nature gives all goods to all men in common; for God has created all things so that all men may enjoy them in common. Thus it was Nature that gave the right to common enjoyment, while it was unjust usurpation that originated the rights of property."

Says Rollins' "Ancient History" (London edition, Vol. 4, page 312):

"For over two hundred years all Christians were communists, who held the land and waters, as well as all timbers and precious metals, in common. There were no superior ecclesiastics among them. The lot was cast in deciding all questions, and the assembled commune judged all disputes; and when any decision was not well pleasing, the whole community passed on it and reversed or confirmed it according to the will of all. This bold democracy was an inheritance from the Jews, and was held in abhorrence by pagans who trafficked in land and made profits from others' labor."

The Danish scholar and Socialist, Dr. Gustav Bang, in his "Crises in European History," writes:

"Christiantity, in its first and purest form, was a religion for the proletariat, for the poor, suffering and oppressed in society. These were the people to whom Christ spoke. . . . . It was the common people that gathered around him and listened to him. His apostles were poor fishermen and artisans, and great was the anger and indignation of the pillars of society, the pharisees and scribes, because publicans and sinners kept close to him to hear him. It was just the miserable and despised people who sought refuge with him, and found not only consolation for the soul but also practical defense against those who were hard on them. The story of the woman caught in adultery is in its sublime simplicity the most scathing expression of contempt for the existing moral hypocrisy, and the answer he gave applies as strongly today: 'He that is without sin among you, let him cast a stone at her.' "

Dr. Bang might well have added that the words reputed to have been spoken by Jesus were also a "most scathing expression of contempt" for Jehovah and his savage scriptural law that commanded that such a woman be publicly stoned to death.

"It was," says this writer, "a decided proletarian tendency which dominated Christianity in the first centuries of our era, *a tendency which theology of later times only succeeded in misrepresenting by sophistically exercising a most reckless violence against the old traditions.* And just as proletarian was the positive social ideal which Christianity proclaimed. It was the communism of property and consumption, the communistic form of society which was the natural expression of the social longings of the ancient proletariat, and which in the first Christian congregations was not only proclaimed but practiced."

Roman society was rotten to the core. The Empire "could not check the process of decay. Social misery grew, and mysticism increased correspondingly." Describing the times Dr. Bang writes:

"A saviour was dreamt of, one who should come and redeem humanity through supernatural means, and it was for a time believed that the first emperors should accomplish this. Their persons were regarded as superhuman, as divine, and many prodigious things were related about them. A comet appeared after Caesar's funeral; it was the soul of the deceased ascending to heaven, the abode of the gods."

Of the ignorant and superstitious condition of the Roman populace of the period, and the source from which sprang the miracles and sorceries found in the New Testament, Dr. Bang writes:

"We find in those days a myriad of unusual conceptions which everywhere were reflections of diseased social conditions. Seers, fortunetellers and conjurers found a large and ever increasing clientele; in all different happenings were seen forebodings of coming events. It is interesting to note how, in the popular belief, things happened which are parallel to many of the miracles mentioned in the New Testament. It was told how divine beings begat children with earthly women, and also how holy men ascended to heaven without leaving a trace of their bodies. There were wonderful cures related of the lame becoming active and the blind gaining their sight. Even the sober historian Tacitus describes how the Emperor Vespasian cured a blind man by moistening his eyes with saliva. They told of awakening of the dead. The famous miracle-worker Apollonius met a funeral procession bringing the corpse of a young woman to the grave; he commanded them to leave the litter on the ground and promised to change their sorrow into joy, and as he touched the dead and uttered some unintelligible words, the young woman arose, spoke, and went back to her parents' house. Significant is it to note that the early Christians did not in the least question the ability of the pagan 'magician' to perform miracles, but they ascribed it to the influence of the devil and evil spirits."

It was from ignorance, not "divine inspiration," that the creed of Constantine sprang. The only "miracle" about it is that it finds acceptance in modern times. As the authority quoted puts it: "Rome had again become the great international exploiter, just as it had been fifteen centuries previously. And the Christian teachings which originally had been the religion of the exploited masses, the poor and oppressed, had become an instrument for the exploitation of the entire world."

It was the Jewish followers of Jesus, called Nazarenes,

that most heroically struggled to free the slaves and revolutionize society. The Roman converts fast fell a prey to the fables of Paul. Says Gibbon (Decline and Fall of the Roman Empire) :

"The Jewish converts, or, as they were afterwards called, the Nazarenes, who had laid the foundations of the Church, soon found themselves overwhelmed by the increasing multitudes, that from all the various religions of polytheism enlisted under the banner of Christ."

The final extinction of the Nazarenes is thus described by the historian quoted:

"At length, under the reign of Hadrian (second century), the desperate fanaticism of the Jews filled up the measure of their calamities; and the Romans, exasperated by their repeated rebellions, exercised the rights of victory with unusual rigor. The emperor founded, under the name of Aelia Capitolina, a new city on Mount Zion, to which he gave the privileges of a colony; and denouncing the severest penalties against any of the Jewish people who should dare to approach its precincts, he fixed a vigilant garrison of a Roman cohort to enforce the execution of his orders. The Nazarenes had only one way to escape the common proscription * * * they elected Marcus for their bishop, a prelate of the race of the Gentiles, and most probably a native either of Italy or some of the Latin provinces."

Thus did the revolutionary religion of Jesus, as maintained by his Jewish followers, fall into the hands of the pagans. Christianity became a mixture of paganism and Paulism.

The Nazarenes repudiated Paul as an impostor. He could not teach among the Jews. He only found a reception among the Greek and Roman mythologists. Bronson C. Keeler, in his "History of the Bible," says:

"In those days Paul was not recognized as a lawful teacher of Christianity, nor was he for more than a hundred years after his death. Paul asked, Am I not an apostle? And the others said he was not." "Paul's early spirit as a prosecutor appears when he wishes that those anti-Paulines who troubled the Galatians were cut off (Gal. V, 12). He once met Peter in Antioch, and an open conflict occurred (Gal. II, 11-12). The Ebionites, one of the most powerful of the early sects, rejected Paul, and said he was an apostate. The Clementine Homilies attack him bitterly under the name of Simon Magus. They reject his Epistles entirely. Justin Martyr rejected him, and scarcely deigned to notice his writings. Hegesippas would not use his Epistles, and said, substantially, that he had falsified Scripture."

Thus perished the message of peace and brotherhood as taught by the Jewish Carpenter of Nazareth, and so was prepared the way for Constantine's final and complete paganizing of the religion of the Nazarenes; and Christianity was made into a mythology as acceptable to the ruling class as was the mythology that preceded it, and from which it was patterned.

The doctrine of a trinity of supreme gods already existed among the ancients. It was the Osiris, Athor and Isis of the Egyptians, and Gibbon presents it as part of the teachings of Plato. He says:

"The three archical or original principles were represented in the Platonic system as three Gods, united with each other by a mysterious and ineffable generation; and the Logos was particularly considered under the more accessible character of the Son of an Eternal Father, and the Creator and Governor of the world."

Imbued with these teachings of Plato, the Gnostics, one of the Christian sects, taught an entirely different theory of Christ's appearance on earth than the story of the virgin birth. They declared, records Gibbon, "that, instead of issuing from the womb of the Virgin, he (Christ) had descended on the banks of the Jordan, in the form of perfect manhood; that he had imposed on the senses of his enemies, and of his disciples; and that the ministers of Pilate had wasted their impotent rage on an airy phantom, who *seemed* to expire on the cross, and, after three days, to rise from the dead."

This is just as reasonable as the story of a virgin conceiving by a ghost, and much more respectable.

Neither story, however, bears as much evidence of truth as the account of the birth of Jesus found in one of the expurgated gospels of the early centuries, and which account, moreover, is confirmed in the book "Sepher Toldoth Jeschua," and which says: "Josephus Pandera, the Roman officer of a Calabrian legion which was in Judea, seduced Miriam of Bethlehem, and was the father of Jesus."

Little, however, did Constantine and his clericals care regarding the myths concerning Christ. It was a religion of submission to the powers that be that Rome purposed to promulgate. Paul had written into the Christian religion the servile injunction, "Let every soul be subject unto the higher powers. For there is no power but of God; the powers that be are ordained by God. Whosoever therefore resisteth the power, resisteth the ordinance of God; and they that resist shall receive to themselves damnation" (Romans, Chapter XIII).

Constantine discovered these words of Paul, and they suited his purposes to a dot.

To again quote Gibbon:

"The passive and unresisting obedience, which bows under the yoke of authority, or even of oppression, must have appeared, in the eyes of an absolute monarch, the most conspicuous and useful of the evangelic virtues. The primitive Christians derived the institution of civil government, not from the consent of the people, but from the decrees of heaven. The reigning emperor (Constantine), though he had usurped the sceptre by treason and murder, immediately assumed the sacred character of vicegerent of the Deity. To the Deity alone he was accountable for the abuse of his power; and his subjects were indissolubly bound, by their oath of fidelity, to a tyrant, who had violated every law of nature and society."

Stripped of its cant and hypocrisy, the Christian religion stands forth as an institution sanctified and purposed to hold the masses in submission to the powers that be. Its god sits on a golden throne in the skies, and ordains all the lords of exploitation and war; and they that resist this god and his ordained earthly lords,

declares St. Paul, "receive to themselves damnation."
With its miserable promise of salvation to slaves and
craven threat of damnation to rebels, the Christian religion is the world's champion of the exploiting classes.
Its god, Jehovah, dragged out of the stone-age, is the
best friend of tyrants among all the gods ever conceived
in the brains of savages. For centuries the creed of
Constantine reigned supreme. To even express a doubt
of its divine origin meant imprisonment and death. The
most hideous instruments of torture that the priests
could conceive awaited those that dared to revolt against
superstition and slavery. Of this reign of papal Rome
Ernst Haeckel says:

"It meant death to all freedom of mental life, decay
to all science, corruption to all morality. * * * With all
the discipline of the church and the fear of God, the
condition of European society was pitiable. Feudalism,
serfdom, the grace of God, and the favor of the monks
ruled the land; the poor helots were only too glad to be
permitted to raise their miserable huts under the shadow
of the castle or the cloister, their secular and spiritual
oppressors and exploiters. Even today we suffer from
the aftermath of these awful ages and conditions, in
which there was no question of care for science or higher
mental culture save in rare circumstances and in secret.
Ignorance, poverty and superstition combined with the
immoral operation of the law of celibacy, which had
been introduced in the eleventh century, to consolidate
the ever-growing power of the papacy. It has been cal-
culated that there were more than ten million victims of

fanatical religious hatred during this 'Golden Age' of papal domination; and how many more million human victims must be put to the account of celibacy, oral confession, and moral restraint, the most pernicious and accursed institutions of the papal depotism!"

"I used to read in books," says Robert G. Ingersoll, "how our fathers persecuted mankind. But I never appreciated it. I read it, but it did not burn itself into my soul. I did not really appreciate the infamies that have been committed in the name of religion until I saw the iron arguments that Christians used. I saw the 'thumb-screw'—two little pieces of iron, armed on the inner surfaces with protuberances to prevent their slipping; through each end a screw uniting the two pieces. And when some man denied the efficacy of baptism, or maybe said, 'I do not believe that a fish ever swallowed a man to keep him from drowning;' then they put his thumb between these pieces of iron, and in the name of universal love and forgiveness began to screw these pieces together. When this was done most men said, 'I will recant.' The man who would not recant was not forgiven. They screwed the thumbscrews down to the last pang, and then threw their victim into some dungeon, where, in the throbbing silence and darkness, he might suffer the agonies of the fabled damned. This was done in the name of love—in the name of mercy—in the name of the compassionate Christ. I saw, too, what they called the 'collar of torture.' Imagine a circle of iron, and on the inside a hundred points almost as sharp as needles. This argument was fastened about the throat of the sufferer. Then he could not walk, nor sit down, nor stir, without the neck being punctured by these points. In a little while the throat would begin to swell, and suffocation would end the agonies of that man. This man, it may be, had committed the crime of saying, with tears upon his cheeks, 'I do not believe that God, the father of us all, will damn to eternal perdition any of the children of men.' I saw another instrument, called the 'scavenger's daughter.' Think of a pair of shears with handles not only where they now are, but at the points as well, and just above the pivot that unites the blades a circle of iron. In the upper handles the hands would be placed; in the lower, the feet; and through the ring at the center the head of the victim would be forced. In this condition he would be thrown prone upon the earth, and the strain upon the muscles produced such agony that insanity would in pity end his pain. I saw the 'rack.' This was a box like the bed of a wagon, with a windlass at each end, with levers and ratchets to prevent slipping; over each windlass went chains; some were fastened to the ankles of the sufferer; others to his wrists. And then priests, clergymen, divines, saints, began turning these windlasses, and kept turning until the ankles, the knees, the hips, the shoulders, the elbows, the wrists of the victim were all dislocated and the sufferer was wet with the sweat of agony. And they had standing by a physician to feel his pulse. What for? To save his life? Yes. In mercy? No; simply that they might rack him once again."

And in Lecky's "Rise of Rationalism" we read:

"Tortures of hell, the whole intellect of Europe was employed in illustrating them. All literature, all painting, all eloquence was concentrated upon the same dreadful theme. By the pen of Dante and by the pencil of Orcagna, by the pictures that crowded every church and the sermons that rang from every pulpit the maddening terror was sustained. The saint was often permitted in visions to behold the agonies of the lost and to recount the spectacle he had witnessed. He loved to tell how by the lurid glare of the eternal flames he had seen mil·lions writhing in every form of ghastly suffering, their eyeballs rolling with unspeakable anguish, their limbs gashed and mutilated and quivering with pain, tortured by pangs that seemed ever keener by the recurrence, and shrieking in vain for mercy to an unpitying heaven. Hideous beings of dreadful and fantastic forms hovered around, mocking them and their torments, casting them into caldrons of boiling brimstone or inventing new tortures more subtle and more refined. Amid this a sulphur stream was always seething, feeding and intensifying the waves of fire. There was no respite, no alleviation, no hope. The tortures were ever varied in their character and they never palled for a moment upon the sense. Sometimes it was said the flames while retaining their intensity withheld the light. A shroud of darkness covered the scene, but a ceaseless shriek of anguish attested the agonies that were below."

Plato, in his "Republic," wrote 400 years before the birth of Jesus:

"And then there are quacks and soothsayers who

flock to the rich man's door, and try to persuade him that they have a power at command, which they procure from heaven, and which enables them, by sacrifices and incantations performed amidst feasting and indulgences, to make amends for any crimes committed either by the individual himself or any of his ancestors; and that should he desire to do a mischief to anyone, it may be done at a trifling expense, whether the object of his hostility be a just or an unjust man, for they profess that by certain invocations and spells, they can prevail upon the gods to do their bidding. And they produce a host of books written by Marseus and Orpheus, children, as they say, of Selene and of the Muses, which form their ritual—persuading not individuals merely, but whole cities also, that men may be absolved and purified from crimes, both while they are still alive and even after their decease, by means of certain sacrifices and pleasurable amusements which they call mysteries, which deliver us from torments of the other world, while the neglect of them is punishable with an awful doom."

Besides the burnings at the stake, the agonies of the rack and torture, who can estimate the mental anguish that the orthodox Christian religion has caused! To this day the Catholic and the Protestant clergy cram their lies of devils and damnation into the brains of little children. The creed of Constantine, with its savage nightmares of a savage god whose wrath against mankind, because a mythical Adam ate a forbidden apple, was only appeased by the bloody sacrifice of his own son, with its devils and torments to curse every creature who does not believe it, is the most hideous religion that was ever spawned in the brains of barbarians.

Under the creed of Constantine the powers of the popes grew until they equalled those attributed to their fabled god himself. The popes became Jehovah's vicegerents, and crowned and uncrowned kings. The papal chair became the most coveted prize in Europe. "Make me Bishop of Rome," exclaimed Proetextatus, a pagan prefect of that city, "and I'll be a Christian too!" It was such a sinecure that rival parties fought for its possession. "In the course of the sixth century," writes Dowling in his "History of Romanism," "the city of Rome thrice witnessed the disgraceful spectacle of rival pontiffs, with fierce hatred, bloodshed and massacre, contending with each other for the spiritual throne." From the sixth century on the creed of Constantine held undisputed sway over Europe. With its root firmly set in the rottenness and depravity of the Dark Ages, the branches of the Upas tree of orthodox Christianity have spread their poisonous shadows over the western world to this very hour. Not a war-lord of Europe but sits on his bloody throne ordained by the Christian God. Not a plutocrat in Christendom but holds his power to exploit the people by the grace of the creed of Constantine. It was for this purpose that the creed of Constantine was conceived, and it has well served its purpose.

"The Church," declares Macauley, "is the handmaid of tyranny and the steady enemy of liberty."

The first master class that history records was the old patriarch. Religion and legend have painted him a holy man and a hero. He was nothing of the kind—he was a holy fright and a bully. He gobbled up all the real estate he could lay his hands on and called it his. He owned it because he took it. He also owned everything that lived or grew upon it. He owned his women and his cattle. He owned his goats and he owned his own offspring. He swapped his cows, or his women and children with his brother patriarch on the next ranch whenever he saw a good trade. He did all this because he was big, and could whip any other man that disputed his right and title. It was wrong for a Jewish patriarch to own a slave born of his own blood, except for a limited number of years, but it was all right to capture and, own a heathen. It appears perfectly proper to some of us, even to this day, to benevolently assimilate a heathen that is weaker than we are. As far as the women were concerned, the Jewish patriarch, like his Gentile brother, classed them with the cattle. To the patriarch the only creature on earth worthy of any respect was his oldest, son by his favorite wife.

Among the Gentiles, when the patriarch died the oldest son fell heir to the entire estate, lands, cattle, women and children—his own mother, together with his father's other wives and concubines, and his own brothers and sisters and half brothers and sisters included. All the lands and herds were his property, and all the human beings were his slaves. If the oldest son, who became the patriarch at the death of his father, inherited more slaves—his own brothers and sisters included—than he needed, he traded part of them for cattle, or sold them.

If he could not trade or sell them, he killed off such as he did not need. Plutarch graphically describes this killing of slaves. There was no hope of freedom for any of the children of these slaves. The law of primogeniture—the inheritance by the oldest son of all the property of the patriarch—was absolute. It was not only embodied in the social law, but was also part of their religion. It was backed by the divine approval as well as the club.

This social system of master and slave, dating back to the earliest times, going through various changes of society from barbarism to organized kingdoms, finally culminated in the western world in the Roman Empire. Under the rule of Rome the master and slave system reached its most diabolical perfection. The patriarch became the patrician of divine origin, and the slave became the brute in human form without a soul. There is nothing as savage in history as Rome. It still rules. It is the full fruition of the curse of master and slave that formed early society. It operates to this day every government and rules every religious organization.

It was into this Roman world of master and slave that Jesus came with a message of human brotherhood. He was a carpenter, born of the outraged working class. Like thousands of rebel slaves before him, his life ended upon a cross. His gospel of redemption from the rule of human monsters, his vision of fraternity and equality, sank deep into the hearts of his Jewish followers, and after his tragic death they heroically labored to lift the people from bondage. They, too, were martyred by

Rome. But the message took root among the oppressed, and for three hundred years struggled and grew. Then Rome accomplished by cunning what it had failed to do by force and murder, and made a state religion of the revolutionary gospel of Jesus. The message of Jesus struggled for existence to the fourth century, and then died, and has been dead as a door nail ever since.

Rome took the simple Jewish carpenter, with his sweet message of human brotherhood, and blatantly deified its own savage murder upon the cross and made of Jesus a tortured god, and placed him in a niche beside her other pagan myths. Paganism today, split into three divisions—three colossal humbugs—viz.: Roman Catholicism, Greek Catholicism, and Protestantism, all offer an outraged world of masters and slaves a creed that for nineteen centuries has filled the earth with exploitation and war, with millionaire and pauper, with cunning and cruelty, with every abomination imaginable, and without even a pretense of proclaiming the brotherhood of man that Jesus taught, the only possible redemption and salvation of the race.

Jesus, who came voicing the democracy of Solon and Isaiah, has been made the bloody sacrifice to a savage god, the scapegoat for human tyrants and money-lords to load their sins on. Just as the cry of the Hebrew prophets was drowned by the trumpets and rituals of the time-serving Hebrew priests, so has been the cry of the Nazarene silenced by the creed-mumbling priests and preachers. Like the old paganism from which it sprang, so has so-called Christianity taught and upheld the system of one class riding upon the back of another as divine. This system, this curse, is taught as a righteous thing and ordained of God. Only a race that had been degraded for ages by the old savage patriarchal society, that made the oldest son by the favorite wife a lord and master over all, would have ever tolerated the tyrannical doctrine of "servants, be obedient to your masters," that for centuries has held the only useful element in society—the working class—in chains. Our government and our religion are ordained by and for the master class. The rulers and the reverends draw both their inspiration and their salaries from the same source —from the money-lords, the lineal descendants of the old patriarchs. There are scholars in the pulpits today who are utterly ashamed of the miserable deception that the creed of Constantine has perpetrated upon the race. Our society, both social and religious, is pagan to the core. Outside of a commonwealth of human brotherhood there is nothing worthy of the name of either religion or state, and before the world-wide sweep of this coming society all tyranny and humbuggery must fall.

For his seditious teachings Jesus was crucified by the Roman rulers, assisted by the time serving priests and the aristocracy of Jerusalem. Crucifixion was the death penalty inflicted by Rome upon rebellious slaves. The Jews never practiced it. None but rebellious slaves were nailed to the cross.

It is an infamous lie to charge the Jewish people with this crime. It was Imperial Rome that murdered Jesus —the same Imperial Rome that years after his death transformed his gospel of peace and brotherhood into the myths that are offered as Christianity today. Roman priests, steeped with the mythologies of Roman paganism, gradually developed our New Testament, and wrote into it the bloody doctrine of the sacrifice of his own son by a blood-thirsty god. Nothing could be more abhorrent to Jesus than the religion offered in his name. It was ordained at the Council of Nice to hold the revolting slaves in order. The vision of brotherhood on earth was removed to another world, and slaves were taught contentment with their lot here, and obedience to their masters, in order that they might live in mansions after they died. Implicit faith in the fall of Adam, the resulting curse, and the wiping away of their sins by the divinely ordained sacrifice of a god, was offered in the place of the glad tidings of brotherhood that Jesus taught. The doctrine of the trinity—three gods in one—was a compromise between the many gods of Rome and the one god of the Jews. The conception of a universal Fatherhood, with its natural complement of a universal Brotherhood, as conceived by Jesus, was hidden beneath the pagan conception of gods and emperors, sitting upon golden thrones in the skies, that rewarded or damned according to the set rules concocted by the priests. Orthodox Christianity became, therefore, a simple thing to accept—all the poor victim had to do in order to believe it was to let others do his thinking. This, sad to relate, has never been a hard thing for the masses to do.

The church stands with the master class, because it

was conceived in the interests of the master class. The church spurns "peace on earth, toward men good will," and upholds war, because the master class, in its game of exploiting the workers, must have wars. The church offers ceremonies, symbols and superstitions to believe, and pagan deities to adore, instead of Brotherhood and Peace to live, and a Universal Source of all life to accept, because the belief in ceremonies, symbols and superstitions, and the adoration of a mythical trinity of royal deities, can chain the workers, both bodily and mentally, while Brotherhood and Peace would set them free. If there were such a thing in existence as a personal devil, he could have quit work and retired to a life of ease long ago—the creed of Constantine has attended well and faithfully to all his dirty work.

Jesus portrayed this life as a preparation of a life to come. We must live as brothers now, in order to be fit citizens of eternity. It is passing strange that so appropriate a preparation and social life should have been so pointedly overlooked by the church all these years. And now that the Socialists are demanding this life on earth of justice and human brotherhood—demanding it even though there were no hereafter—they are called enemies of religion!

"Pure paganism," says Osborne Ward in his "Ancient Lowly," "was that of the idea of an aristocratic religion whose priesthood was a part of the state government. It denied the equality of men. It strenuously upheld and stubbornly contended for the divinity of rights—a divinity that was based on the august power of the paternal despot, and still adheres in the form of the aged law of inheritance and the rule of entailments upon primogeniture, or a species of godhead for the first-born son, and in the inheritance of living monarchs. * * * It was a despotism of masters over slaves, which despised the laborers, originally its own children, while it feasted upon their works."

Rome and all that is allied to Rome, ecclesiastical or political, is the most bitter enemy of humanity in all the universe. Socially and religiously the world is pagan.

CHAPTER V

ITS power shattered in western Europe by the flood of modern science, the creed of Constantine is making its last stand on American soil. It is allied with the most powerful money monopoly that ever held a people in bondage. The political powers of America, the pliant tools of the financial corporations that control the industries of the nation, are the agents and allies of the creed that has ruled and ruined the race for centuries. The exploiters of America have made a covenant with Rome in order to subject the masses to more helpless and hopeless bondage and hold themselves more securely in power. Well do they realize that their interests are safe if the Roman Church can rule. At the conclave of Roman prelates held in the city of Boston, in October, 1913, the proposition was boldly proclaimed as to Rome's purpose. At this conclave, and reported in the Boston Journal of October 20, 1913, Rt. Rev. M. F. Fallon, D. D., Bishop of London, Ontario, said: "We propose to make North America Catholic; to bring America to Christ through the divine doctrines of the Catholic

Church and under the supreme shepherdship of the Pope of Rome."

That the money power of America makes no bones of its covenant with this conspiracy is witnessed in the utterances of its political mouthpieces. Said Harper's Weekly, editorially:

"There is ground for thinking that the disposition of civilized mankind to desire the upholding of Catholicism as a force conducive to the commonwealth is likely to wax rather than to wane. From both a religious and an economic point of view the Catholic Church is coming to be regarded as a sheet-anchor of society. Where else is there to be found a rampart against skepticism on the one hand and against Socialism on the other?"

And the Los Angeles Times has declared:

"The Catholic Church in America stands like a stone wall against anarchy and Socialism and the divorce evil, and it always upholds law and order. For these reasons alone no right minded American can find cause for alarm in the growth of the Catholic Church in this country, no matter what church he may belong to himself."

The Outlook says:

"But America today stands in peculiar need of that contribution which the Roman Catholic Church is peculiarly fitted to furnish. For the chief peril to America is from disorganizing forces and a lawless spirit. One of the chief lessons Americans need to learn is reverence for constituted authority and willing obedience to law. This lesson the Roman Catholic Church is peculiarly fitted to teach. That church is a vast spiritual police force, a protection of society from the mob; wherever it goes it teaches submission to control, and that is the first step toward that habit of self-control in the individual which is an indispensable condition of self-government in the community."

To show that the money power of America is today united, whether Catholic, Protestant or Jewish, and are all agreed that the old Roman Catholic Church is the only dependable power to rule the country, read the following from the Jewish organ, The Federation Review:

"As regards the Catholics, moreover, let us not forget that they well nigh constitute the backbone of our fighting forces on sea and land and the upholders of law and order in our cities and villages. It is an open truth that the Catholics furnish the largest proportion of our blue-coats, bluejackets and boys in khaki."

The press of America is dominated by the money kings; it voices their sentiments in its columns. Nor need any one dream that Rome has changed her brutal creed and bloody ways. The Rome that slaughtered Francisco Ferrer in Spain, that murdered the Maderos in Mexico, would butcher its way into power in America at any moment it had the chance. Papal Rome slaughtered Ferrer because he advocated modern schools in Spain, and the same Papal Rome declares its intention to outlaw the public schools of America. . In the name of its creed Rome considers any means justifiable, and still has the thumbscrew and rack, the torture and the stake up its pagan sleeves. "The Socialists should be silenced by a bullet," shrieks the Roman Catholic priest, J. L. Belford, of New York—and the Dark Age bigots that would murder Socialists would just as soon murder free thinkers, or any others that would not bow to papal power.

From the Council of Nice, the gloom began to settle upon Europe; and when Charlemagne, who had reduced nearly all Europe under his sway, went to Rome, in the month of November, in the year 800, and there made compact with the church that recognized the pope as God Himself on earth, ruler of all mankind, and on Christmas Day was crowned by the pope as Emperor of the Romans, popery went forth to rule, and the world's midnight began.

When Rome ruled there were no public schools—ignorance is Rome's bulwark. And the same Rome that boasts it will rule America, anathematizes our public schools. Rome would not have you to turn to scholars for knowledge; she commends you to go to dead saints. Rome bids you to look to beads instead of science for help.

We talk of "our liberty," and have well nigh forgotten that its price is eternal vigilance. If Rome ruled America, as it avows it will, do you doubt but that its Roman ruled courts would be a repetition of the old Inquisition? Rome cannot rule—it knows no other way—save by force and ignorance. When the ignorance fails—when a man dares to think for himself—then the force must be used. How long, do you think, with America under the power of the pope, would it be before the people, with raised hands, would be compelled to take the oath they used to take:

"I swear by God and Holy Mary and by the sign of the cross and the words of the holy gospel, that I will favor and defend and assist the Holy Catholic faith and the Holy Inquisition, its officers and ministers, and that I will declare and discover all heretics whatsoever, abettors, defenders, and concealers of them, disturbers and obstructors of the said Holy Office, and that I will not give them favor, nor help, nor concealment; but that immediately that I know them I will reveal and denounce them to the senors inquisitors; and should I act differently may God so punish me as those deserve who willfully perjure themselves."

"One of the chief lessons Americans need to learn is reverence for constituted authority," says the Outlook, mouthpiece of the powers that be; and the "constituted authority" in America is the money power. "This lesson" of "reverence" to the self-constituted authority of wealth "the Roman Catholic Church is peculiarly fitted to teach," continues the Outlook. No doubt of it. The past history of the Roman Church amply testifies to her "peculiar fitness" to do any bloody work tyrants may want done in order to subject the people. It is this recognized "peculiar fitness" on the part of Rome that is causing the exploiters and politicians of America to ally themselves with the Catholic Church. They know the harlot like a book—and they know she can be trusted to rule with an iron fist. They know her past history.

Lea, in his "History of the Inquisition in Spain," tells how the courts were run. He says:

"The inquisitors, of course, were the superior officials of the tribunal. They were the judges, with practically unlimited power over the lives and fortunes and honor of all whom they summoned before them, until they were gradually restricted by the growing centralization of the Supreme Council. To the people they were the incarnation of the dreaded Holy Office, regarded with more fear and veneration than bishop or noble, for all the powers of church and state were placed at their disposal. They could arrest and imprison at will; with their excommunication they could, at a word, paralyze the arm of all secular officials, and, with their interdict (the cessation of religious privileges), plunge whole communities into despair. Such a concentration of secular and spiritual authority, guarded by so little limitation and responsibility, has never, under any other system, been entrusted to fallible human nature."

Do you imagine for a moment that the exploiters of America would not endorse the methods that Rome is so skilled in? The exploiters of America, who control the government and the courts, employ themselves the same sort of bloody methods to maintain their power. When the workers in any industrial center strike for a little more of the wealth they produce by their labor, for shorter hours and more humane conditions, these exploiters, through the government they control *by the vote of the workers,* send their armed thugs and shoot men, women and children of the working class as ruthlessly and brutally as Rome ever did when in power. But they feel that their hold on the people is weakening, that the workers are fast awakening, and so plutocracy, fearful of its future safety, turns for help to its ancient para- mour, the Church of Rome. Plutocracy hopes that there is sufficient superstition still afflicting the suffering slaves to put the conspiracy across. Plutocracy wants the Church of Rome to rule the brains of the people, so that it can better pick their pockets. Plutocracy that robs the cra- dles and puts babies to work in its mills does not give a damn about saving the peoples' souls—it's the product of the people's labor that it wants to "save," for itself. And the Roman Church is only too willing to assist in this work.

The "Little Treasure of Prayers," a prayerbook used by the Lutheran Church, discloses how bitterly anything that appears like freedom and fraternity is opposed by orthodox Protestants, as well as Catholics. The book has different styles of prayers specially designed for peo- ple occupying different stations in life. It has prayers for husbands and prayers for wives, and it has a prayer for servants. The "Prayer of a Servant" is found on page 32 of the American edition. As the creed of Con- stantine is intended to make the servants contented with their earthly lot, this prayer is most important. After praising the mercy of God because he had his son sac- rificed to save sinners, this "Prayer of a Servant" pro- ceeds as follows: "I pray thou wouldst in mercy grant, that I may not conceive a dislike to my calling of bodily service, into which thou hast placed me according to thy will and good pleasure, and that I may not impatiently rebel against thy order, nor begrudge other people their higher station, but that I may obey Thy will with a cheerful heart, and that I do not regard it otherwise than that I were serving Thee, O God in heaven, and not men on earth."

Isn't it comforting for a servant to feel he is working his head off for God, and not for his earthly master!

This prayer, bear in mind, is not intended for the master to use—it is only for the "lower classes" who do the work of the world.

No master is ever expected to pour forth any such supplication as this.

After the servant has told the Lord how happy he or she is because his or her soul has been saved by the master's God, even if his or her body is exploited to the limit on earth, this prayer goes on to petition that the servant may be "obedient in all things" to the "master and mistress, according to the flesh, not only to them that are kind and lenient, but also to them who are rude and froward, serving them with patience, in all fear and simplicity of heart."

This kind of prayer is guaranteed to keep the servant from voting the Socialist ticket.

Here is some more, found in this prayer: "Preserve unto me good health, strengthen the members of my body and increase my powers; * * * that I may be able to perform the labor of my master and mistress, to improve their property by Thy divine help."

The "servant," it will be noted, does not pray for good

health and stout limbs in order to enjoy these blessings for himself, but that he may be able to work harder and longer hours for the master and "improve his property." What a happiness this is for both the one that does the work and the one that does the exploiting!

Here is a sample of the literature that the priests are pouring into the innocent minds of the children of Ireland. It is taken from a penny pamphlet called "The Sight of Hell," which is one of a series of Roman Catholic religious "Books for Children and Young Persons," written by the Rev. J. Furniss, and published by James Duffy & Co., 1 Wellington Quay, Dublin. It has the approval of the pope, for it contains the printed "imprimatur"— "Permissu Superiorum." Listen to some of the threats contained in this book "for children," written by Priest Furniss, with the papal approval:

"Look into this room. What a dreadful place it is! The roof is red-hot, the walls are red-hot, the floor is like a thick sheet of red-hot iron. See, on the middle of that red-hot floor stands a girl. She looks about sixteen years old. Her feet are bare, she has neither shoes nor stockings on her feet; her bare feet stand on the red-hot burning floor. The door of this room has never been opened before since she first set her feet on the red-hot floor.

"Now she sees that the door is opening. She rushes forward. She has gone down on her knees on the red-hot floor. Listen! She speaks. She says: 'I have been standing with my bare feet on this red-hot floor for years. Day and night my only standing place has been this red-hot floor. Sleep never came to me for a moment that I might forget this horrible burning floor. Look,' she says, 'at my burnt and bleeding feet. Let me go off this burning floor for one moment, only for one single moment. Oh, that in this endless eternity of years I might forget the pain only for one single moment.'

"The devil answers her question: 'Do you ask,' he says, 'for a moment, for one moment, to forget your pain? No; not for one single moment during the never-ending eternity of years shall you ever leave this red-hot floor!'

" 'Is it so?' the girl says, with a sigh that seems to break her heart. 'Then, at least, let somebody go to my little brothers and sisters who are alive and tell them not to do the bad things which I did, so they will never have to come and stand on the red-hot floor.'

"The devil answers again: 'Your little brothers and sisters have the priests to tell them these things. If they will not listen to the priests, neither would they listen, even if somebody should go to them, from the dead.'

"Oh, that you could hear the horrible, the fearful scream of that girl when she saw the door shutting, never, to be opened any more.

"Look into this little prison. In the middle of it there is a boy, a young man. He is silent; despair is on him. He stands straight up. His eyes are burning like two burning coals. Two long flames come out of his ears. His breathing is difficult. Sometimes he opens his mouth, and breath of blazing fire rolls out of it.

"But listen! There is a sound just like that of a kettle boiling. Is it really a kettle that is boiling? No. Then what is it? Hear what it is. The blood is boiling in the scalded veins of that boy; the brains are bubbling in his head, the marrow is boiling in his bones!

"Ask him, put the question to him, why he is thus tormented? His answer is, that when he was alive, his blood boiled to do very wicked things, and he did them, and it was for that he went to dancing-houses, public-houses and theaters. Ask him, does he think the punishment greater than he deserves? 'No,' he says, 'my punishment is not greater than I deserve, it is just. I knew it not so well on earth, but I know now that it is just. There is a just and a terrible God. He is terrible to sinners in hell—but he is just!'

"Perhaps at this moment, seven o'clock in the evening, a child is going to hell. Tomorrow evening at seven o'clock, go and knock at the gates of hell and ask what the child is doing. The devils will go and look. Then they will come back again and say, the child is burning! Go in a week and ask what the child is doing. You will get the same answer—it is burning! Go in a year and ask; the same answer comes—it is burning! Go in a million years and ask the same question; the answer is just the same—it is burning; so if you go forever and ever, you will always get the same answer, it is burning in the fire!

"Little child, if you go to hell, there will be a devil at your side to strike you. He will go on striking you every minute forever and ever, without ever stopping. The first stroke will make your body as bad.as the body of Job, covered from head to foot with sores and ulcers. The second stroke will make your body twice as bad as the body of Job. The third stroke will make your body three times as bad as the body of Job. The fourth stroke will make your body four times as bad as the body of Job. How, then, will your body be after the devil has been striking it every moment for a hundred million of years without stopping?

"But listen now—listen to the tremendous, the horrible uproar of millions and millions and millions of tormented creatures mad with the fury of hell. Oh, the screams of fear, the groanings of horror, the yells of rage, the cries of pain, the shouts of agony, the shrieks of despair from millions on millions. There you hear them roaring like lions, hissing like serpents, howling like dogs and wailing like dragons. There you hear the gnashing of teeth and the fearful blasphemies of the devils. Above all, you hear the roaring of the thunders of God's anger, which shakes hell to its foundations.

"Let us look at hell once more before we leave it. See that man who has just asked for mercy and could not get it. He cannot bear the scorching fire which burns his body through and through. But he must bear it. On the earth hungry man looks for bread, and at last he gets it. A sick man looks for his pain to be less, and at last it gets less. The man in hell looks for the burning to stop—but it does not stop. Then he begins to think how long will the horrible burning go on. His thoughts go through millions and millions of years that cannot be counted. Will the burning stop then? His understanding tells him, No—never—never—never!"

It is easy to discover where the Protestant high-priced revivalists obtain their theology.

THE nineteenth century is the historic age of industrial and mental revolution. The social revolution of the twentieth century will be the full fruition. The marvelous machines, born of the genius of the working class, have revolutionized production, creating wealth in an abundance never before dreamed of. But these machines, that should prove a blessing, have served but to grind the toilers into harder servitude and deeper poverty, because, from the very nature of our social arrangement, they immediately became the private property of the few who did not create them and are used to exploit the many who both create and operate them. Thus there exists the abnormal and panic generating condition in which the class that uses the machines does not own them, and the class that owns them does not use them. Socialism proposes to reverse this abnormal arrangement. As it was expressed by the Hebrew prophet, "They shall not build, and another inhabit; they shall not plant and another eat."

Our present system of society, that so unjustly arranges its production and distribution of wealth, is the heritage of all former systems. The chattel slave sys-. tem of ancient Rome and the feudal system of later Europe yet instill society with the poison of "class distinctions" and "caste."

Man must learn at last that he can make no laws. He can make mistakes and call them laws and suffer thereby. The physical laws are nature's laws. Congress might pass a decree that you could put your bare hand in a blazing fire, and your hand would not burn; but it would burn just the same. The laws of health are Nature's laws. Find and obey them, and we are well; break them, and we sicken. Man can neither make nor alter these laws. So it is with society. There *are* social laws, and the nations that broke them have perished. We cannot make or change social laws. We can collectively break them and suffer, and finally, by so persisting, commit national suicide. Let us find these laws. Let us apply them as we find them, and LIVE! When we do find them, we will discover that the social laws—the laws that must govern a living society—are founded on absolute Justice. Nothing else can endure. Nothing else is worthy of endurance. This is the message of Socialism.

I do not for a moment ridicule a real religion. I love the Golden Rule, and, to me, Justice between man and man, Brotherhood and Love, are fairer than the golden stars at night. Nor do I deny the immortality of the soul, nor that the Universe itself is planned and guided. I know but little, though, beyond the earth, who is my beautiful Mother, and the blood and breed of the human race. I love these because I see and know them, and I renounce and despise any religion, conceived by any creature, that does not say to every soul, "You have just as good a right upon this earth as any other, and none shall rob you, or degrade you."

Roman society was a system of masters and slaves. Slavery was carried to such an extent that even physicians were owned by their masters. Cruelty, slavery, war— these were the dominant factors of the Roman social system; and, it is needless to remark, these factors still exist.

The slaves were degraded to the fullest extent that the masters could drive them. They were taught that they had no souls; they were looked upon as animals. Today society teaches differently with its lips, but by its acts towards the workers it still patterns after ancient Rome. The city of Athens, the boasted center of culture and learning, at the time of the birth of Jesus, contained 400,000 slaves out of its entire population of 515,000. The city of Corinth, with its population of 640,000, contained only 40,000 free men and women—the remaining 600,000 being slaves. The patrician class claimed to have immortal souls because they were descended from the gods; the slaves had no immortal souls, because they were created by the gods to serve their divine masters. Against this Roman master-and-slave system of society had arisen, prior to the birth of Jesus, revolters among the slaves, who had led numerous but unsuccesful rebellions. Labor unions, meeting in secret, existed as far back as B. C. 600. Despite the fact that crucifixion was the horrible punishment dealt to rebellious slaves, bloody mutinies occurred that bear witness to the class-struggles of ancient society. Among the last of the nations that fell under the power of Rome was Palestine, and, while the Roman yoke fell lightly upon the rich and aristocratic Jews, yet the submission to a Gentile power galled the entire Jewish nation. Therefore with more yearning than ever, and with stronger hope, did the Jews look to a coming Messiah who would overthrow the power of the Caesars and again establish the Jewish kingdom. The cruelty, the savagery of Roman ruled society was at its height when Jesus appeared. Born of the Jewish working class, Jesus grew up amidst the scenes of Roman outrage committed against human flesh and blood. He saw the workers—his own class—in all the torture of Roman bondage. The spirit of revolt welled up in his soul— it became the passion of his life. We are told—and the account so fits his life and character that it is most likely true—that among his first public utterances was the defiant message narrated in the 4th chapter of Luke, and which nearly cost him his life. The account, beginning at the 16th verse of this chapter, reads:

"And he came to Nazareth, where he had been brought up; and, as his custom was, he went into the synagogue on the Sabbath day, and stood up for to read.

"And there was delivered unto him the book of the prophet Isaiah; and when he had opened the book, he found the place where it was written,

"The Spirit of the Lord is upon me, because he hath anointed me to preach the gospel to the poor; he hath sent me to heal the broken-hearted, to proclaim deliverance to the captives, and recovering of sight to the blind, to set at liberty them that are bruised (enslaved)."

And then, we are told, Jesus closed the scroll and made a talk. It was the old Jewish custom to allow any one to thus discourse in the synagogue. He certainly must have delivered a scathing message, for, the account says, "all they in the synagogue, when they heard these things, were filled with wrath, and thrust him out of the city, and led him unto the brow of the hill whereon their city was built, that they might cast him down headlong." But Jesus made his escape.

With this evidence of the murderous intent on the part of the congregation in the synagogue, it becomes the rankest sort of hypocrisy for the clericals of today to claim that Jesus meant the "captives of sin" that he was preaching deliverance to. No pious Pharisees, ancient or modern, ever threatened the life of anybody who confined his talk of "deliverance" to a "deliverance from sin."

A Boston mob, of the same religious caliber and for the same reason as the ancient mob that dragged Jesus to "the brow of the hill," once put a rope about William Lloyd Garrison's neck and proposed to hang him because William Lloyd Garrison also cried that he had come "preaching deliverance to the captives"—the captive negro slaves of the nineteenth century. If William Lloyd Garrison had been nothing but a regulation preacher—a tool of the master-class—and had confined his remarks about saving the poor darkies' lost souls, the pious Boston people would have taken up a collection for him instead of hunting a rope. Jesus meant what he said—his message of redemption to a lost world was human brotherhood, not masters and slaves, and so he cried that he had come to bring "deliverance to the captives." The Roman slaves were well called "captives." They were captured by Roman soldiers from the barbarian tribes at that period of northern Europe, and brought in chains to the cities and sold in the slave marts.

History tells us that not far from the temple in Jerusalem was a Roman slave market where rich Jews could purchase men-servants and maid-servants of "heathen" blood, as Jehovah had told them to do. Probably there were a number of these, owners of "captives," present, when Jesus thundered his defiant message of deliverance to the captives.

They knew what Jesus meant by "deliverance to the captives," even if the modern clergy do not.

And the exploiters and their priests of old Jerusalem did not like Jesus, no more than the exploiters of today like an agitator against wage-slavery. And so, because he was a rebel, because he fearlessly defied the Biblical laws and denounced the rulers and robbers and their high-priests, Jesus met his death upon the cross. Then began a struggle on the part of his Jewish followers to establish a society of freedom and fraternity that is not equalled for devotion and sacrifice in the annals of history. Imperial Rome, with the ferocity of a wild beast, went to work to crush the communist movement of the first century. The followers of Jesus were slaughtered

in every monstrous manner that Rome could conceive.
And still the movement grew. Then began the work to
stem by cunning the revolutionary tide that butchery
could not check. About the first reactionary "convert"
to Christianity that we have any record of was Paul. By
birth, it is said, Paul was half Greek and half Jewish
Pharisee. He was not the first, nor was he the last, to
garble and distort the message of a great prophet of the
people and bury its truths in a heap of myths. Paul
emasculated the glad tidings of Jesus by removing the
kingdom of heaven upon earth, that Jesus visioned, to
some remote locality beyond the stars, after the poor,
suffering "captives" were dead. It did not take the
Roman rulers and their priests long to discover what a
splendid thing it would be to doctor up Paul's myths and
make a "Catholic" faith of them. By the middle of the
third century pagan priests were being converted to
Paul's conception of Christianity in job lots, and
they added to it such devils, torments, rites and
ceremonies as they saw fit. Roman society—a society
of masters and slaves—must have a religion purposely
designed to keep the masses in subjection, and what could
be better for this than a creed that promised eternal
happiness to the faithful, and eternal damnation to the
heretics? It even beat the pagan religion of telling the
slaves they had no souls. Paul's injunction, "Servants,
be obedient to your masters"—giving the direct lie to
Jesus, who said, "Call no man master"—made a splendid
foundation upon which the Roman priests could build a
Catholic—meaning "universal"—faith.

There is no doubt but that Jesus was a spiritualist, not a materialist; he taught immortality and proclaimed that the slaves and their masters were of one blood. But Jesus dwelt but very little upon the hereafter—his message was to establish justice, peace and brotherhood upon earth and that such a just society would naturally be of itself a soul-saving power.

How different is this from the creed of Constantine!

By the beginning of the fourth century Roman priesthood had virtually crushed the revolutionary movement inaugurated by the early followers of Jesus. The Council of Nice, under the authority of Constantine, had canonized such spurious writings of Roman origin as it saw fit, and created the New Testament. From this period began the rapid construction of the Roman Catholic Church; and when the year 800 dawned in Europe, this substitution of the message of Jesus to an enslaved world was clothed with a power outranking all kings and governments.

In the night of papal Rome the libraries of the ancient world are burned. Philosophy is outlawed, art is banished and learning despised. Freedom and fraternity are buried beneath tyranny, class-rule and bigotry. Lies are put into the mouths of gods, and outrages charged to holy ghosts. The search of science becomes a crime, and faith in frauds and fables a virtue. Love is a vice, birth and motherhood a disgrace, and sexual perverts become a saintly sight in the eyes of God.

Never was hatched a more infamous plot than the prostituting of the revolutionary message of the Palestine peasant into the nightmare of Roman Catholicism.

Oh! the irony of fate, that the class that crucified Jesus should in after years boast of the murder, and make the hideous cross a religious symbol, a saving grace for oppressed and outraged humanity!

Is it any wonder that Haeckel has exclaimed: "Unbelieving philosophers, who have collected disproofs of the existence of God, have overlooked one of the strongest arguments in that sense—the fact that the Roman 'Vicar of Christ' could for twelve centuries perpetrate with impunity the most shameful and horrible deeds in the name of God!"

True, in the Old Testament laws the Roman Church could find ample authority to justify every atrocious act, from slavery to bloodshed, that it wished to commit; but the fact remains, to his eternal glory, that Jesus repudiated these biblical injunctions as fearlessly as he did the Roman social system of his day. "It is written an eye for an eye and a tooth for a tooth," says the Bible; "but I say unto you something different—something better"—, spake the free soul of Jesus. For inspiration Jesus went to Israel's martyred prophets, not to Israel's priests and lawgivers. To the visions of Isaiah Jesus turned, not to the book of Leviticus.

The popes of Rome became absolute monarchs of Europe. These self-styled representatives of God lived lives so foul that the story cannot be told in detail; the papal palace became a bawdy house, and bastard popes sat upon the "throne of St. Peter." The feudal barons lorded in wanton luxury over their serfs, safe under the loving care of the Holy Father. Never a serf took to himself a wife, but the baron demanded the right of sleeping the first night with the bride; and the church called this unspeakable outrage the will of God. The chattel slaves of Imperial Rome—the captives that Jesus longed to free—became feudal serfs when Rome ruled the brains and bodies of men.

To this rule of papal Rome the American exploiters look with longing eyes. They would return again to an age when stolen wealth and bloody wars have priestly benediction. The class that drags babies into its mills and factories, that drives maidens into prostitution through starvation wages, that carries on wars abroad and shoots down striking men and women in its industrial centers, views with complacency the thumbscrews and racks, the tortures and fagots ordained to hold the common people in submission. Once more there is knocking at the doors of your hearts the ancient query, "Caesar, or Christ?" Not the pagan Christ of the creed of Constantine, not the mythic god upon a gilded throne, but the Christ of Humanity, the deliverer of the Captives, the Opener of the eyes of the Deluded, the Lover of Labor and the Prophet of Brotherhood and Peace. For nineteen centuries this Christ, this Revolutionary Redeemer from oppression, has been hidden by the church. A world of masters and enslaved workers, a world of wars, a world reeking with poverty and desolation, with agony and tears, has been the answer to Rome's pagan religion. A world of brothers, a world of peace, a world of plenty for all, a world wherein the old shall go down to rest with the sweet music of a life of love lulling them to their last sleep—this is the only religion worth while.

A religion that is real—what a boon that would be to the world! Not a priest-made creed that saves your soul by believing something that isn't so, but a religion of Humanity, of Love, of Peace, of Justice; a religion that would look oppression in the face and smite it; that would curse war and drive the war-demons off the earth; that would demand equality in the means of life, and class a profit-monger with other burglars; that would open wide the gates of Knowledge, Science and Art. To such a religion the workers of all races could come, and throw to the winds the myths and goblins that frighten them, and keep them apart, by cunningly claiming to hold the keys of a mythic heaven and hell.

What mad deities are these that the priests have conceived, that demand you should believe some silly fable or lose your immortal soul! What gods are these, sprung from the brains of bigots, that crave bloody sacrifices and crucified Christs to appease their wrath! And how utterly blind the slaves have been all down the ages not to discern that the fraud was created to hold them in submission to their masters!

What more shameful sight can there be in all the universe than that of creatures worshiping and loving different styles of gods and robbing and fighting and hating each other! A country that legalizes pirates to fence in the land and own the means of life, so that millions are driven to poverty, vice and erime; that drives women and children into its mills and mines and exploits them to the last drop of blood in their worn bodies; a country that has armies and navies and gunmen to murder in order to hold a master-class in power; such a country, and such a people, are afflicted with a religion that befits cannibals.

To think what a beautiful land this might be if Justice was the only creed; what a happy race could journey from the morning of life, down to the shades of night, if Brotherhood was the only confession of faith; what clean souls might possess us, if Love was the only god; to think of this, and then look abroad at a land held in the claws of human hyenas; to gaze upon a race degraded and degenerated by the monsters of mammon; to view such misery and sorrow as would touch a heart of stone; away with the social system and the creed that holds such savagery in power!

And then behold them—the Christians—with the wealth stolen from labor in their pockets, how they walk with heads held high over the human wrecks they have made—how they put in iron cages the victims who have broken Christian laws rather than starve—how they drive from haunt to gutter the women who have sold their virtue to feed their bodies—and then look—they are singing that "Jesus paid it all," "every debt they owe!" They are "washed in the blood of the Lamb," are these exploiters and extortioners, and, while the millions they have outraged and robbed lead tortured earthly lives and go to eternal torment when they die if they do not humbly accept the "Jesus paid it all" creed, they—the sanctified and saved exploiters and extortioners—live lives of luxury here, and go to endless happiness when they leave this world.

Blind faith atrophies the mind; to doubt is the beginning of wisdom.

The only faith worthy a sane soul is faith in whatever appeals to the reason as being true, or at least the most probable. If you think it probable that the Creator of the Universe once told the Jews to slaughter all the Midianites—the men, the old women, and all the innocent children and babes—to slaughter all save the young maidens, and to take these for their own lust, if you think this is even probable, then have faith and believe it. You will find this recorded in the book of Numbers, chapter 31, verse 18. You will also find numerous other horrors told in this book. You will find, in your Bible, polygamy and slavery sanctioned by Jehovah. If you believe these things to be ordinances handed down from a God on a throne, you, according to the church, are full of faith.

For my part, to put it mildly, I claim it is an infamous lie to charge these atrocities to any god—these brutal things were simply done by savages, the same savages that today drag little children into their mills of mammon.

Every ruler in Christendom claims to exist by the grace of God. God is back of them all. He has ordained every crowned head. All rulers—kings, emperors, kaisers and presidents depend alike upon God. Their strength, so they say, is in God, the God Jehovah, who is all-powerful. If this be so, if an all-powerful God is behind the rulers of Christendom, then what need have they of your help? What need have they of armies, if this God is their backer? What need have they of shot and shell if a God that holds the lightnings in his fist is their stronghold? Let the rulers take their God when they go to war—isn't he powerful enough to do the work? What need has a ruler of soldiers armed with swords and guns when God is with him? When the rulers of Christian nations declare war against each other, let them and their God go to it. Let the people stay at home and attend to their own business. It is none of their mix-up. If there is any slaughtering to be done, surely their God is able to do it. What care you which ruler comes out ahead? They are all the same to you, who do the work of the world. Rulers and masters, ordained of God, all exploit you alike. They all live in idle luxury off the labor of the common people. The same God ordains them all to ride on your back. If they quarrel, and want to fight over the plunder, then let them depend upon their God. If their God cannot help them, what good is he? Is their God deaf, dumb, blind and helpless? Is he such a weakling that he and his pets have to depend on soldiers to keep them from tumbling off their seats? Let us find out. Let the common people keep out of the bloody quarrels of the God-ordained rulers, and let the God-ordained rulers depend entirely for help on the God that ordains them. Let them drag out their God from under thrones and behind altars and march him on to war. It is time enough for you to shoot when you see this God coming after you. Don't load your gun for a German or French or English or Italian or Russian workingman—wait till this God shows up.

Maybe you will find out that your rulers, the pickpockets, have lied to you about a God being behind them. Maybe all they can trot out is a phantom of their fabled devil. Anyway, it's well worth finding out.

God's guidance of the world's despots, to hear the despots tell it themselves, is indeed something wonderful. From Moses' slaughter of the Midianites down to the ravishing of Poland and Belgium and Ireland Jehovah's guiding hand is plainly seen. No human would think of committing such atrocities without a God to help him. It was God that had Edith Cavell shot at Brussels. It was God that had hired gunmen butcher the pregnant women and babies at Ludlow. It was God that directed the shells that killed women and children on the streets of Vera Cruz. A wonderful and strange God—especially when we size up the creatures he chooses to do his work. They are tainted with insanity. Some future historian may write a book disclosing how the world for ages mistook insanity for inspiration. The history of the ruling family of Austria—the Hapsburgs—records 853 insane men and women, says Dr. Frederick Adams Woods, of the biological department of the Massachusetts Institute of Technology. The Bourbon family of Spain reeks with insanity back to the days of Pedro the Cruel, who, for amusement, used to rip open the bellies of women and watch them die. One of his illustrious descendants was Queen Joanna the Mad, mother of Charles the V. of Austria and Spain, particular friend and wholesale butcher of the pope's. The Romanoffs of Russia are a race of madmen. From Ivan the Terrible, who murdered his own son, they have produced only assassins and brutes. James the I. of England was known as his "Sowship." King Leopold of Belgium was known all over Europe for his licentious and idiotic performances. And it is such as these that have the help of the Christian God. No doubt of it. St. Paul himself says so—says the demented, degenerate rulers are ordained of God.

The creed of Constantine was concocted, and most of the New Testament written, in the days when there were no printed books, no public schools; when not one in a thousand could read or write. In those days dreams were facts and spasms counted for science. The earth was flat; below it was hell and above it was heaven; the sun was pulled by God from east to west during the day, and was suddenly jerked back to the east some time during the night; and the stars were lanterns that angels held by cords. If a man was sick he was full of devils, and could only be cured by the incantations of a priest. Old and toothless women were hung or burned as witches. To doubt was heresy, punishable by torture and death. If anyone uttered a truth his tongue was pulled out with red-hot pincers. If he didn't then recant he was flayed alive or burned at the stake.

The creed of Constantine is a religion of monstrosities and murder—of insanity, not inspiration.

In the phantasmagorial work of fiction by Edgar Rice Burroughs, "Tarzan of the Apes," it is told of Kerchak, king of the tribe: "Suddenly something snapped in the wicked little brain of the anthropoid. With a frightful roar the great beast sprang among the assemblage. Biting and striking with his huge hands he killed and maimed a dozen ere the balance could escape to the upper terraces of the forest."

Kerchak, king of the great anthropoids, had gone war-mad. Something had snapped in his wicked little brain. The lust to kill was upon him. Kerchak was a patriot of the jungle. And though we of the human breed have left our anthropoidal ancestors far behind, yet the blood of Kerchak of the Apes still, at times, boils in our veins. Suddenly something snaps in wicked little brains, and the lust to kill—the war craze—is upon us. It is everywhere, and all down the ages.

The naked savages are sitting sullenly around the campfire. Suddenly one of the braves arises, and with crouching body, teeth set like a vise, spear deftly poised, slowly begins the war-dance. One after another of the tribe spring to their feet and fall in line; the big medicine man beats the tom-tom; the wild and weird war-song pierces the forest; the tribes of fur and feather flee in terror; the war-dance of the savage is in full blast. The Apache paints his body, puts a plume upon his head and a scalp-belt around his waist, and his preparedness is complete. Something has snapped in his wicked little brain, and he is off to kill.

A home-loving, peaceful people are sitting by their firesides. Suddenly is heard the howl of the politician, the preacher, and the press. Something has snapped in their wicked little brains. The blood of Kerchak of the Apes is rioting in their veins. The madness to kill is upon them. The war-dance of the civilized human be-gins—the Big Preparedness Parade, with brass bands and drums and fluttering flags marches down the streets, and the home-loving, peaceful people fall in line. They are prepared to follow the flag to hell.

Once, we killed for the sheer love of killing. Again, we killed because our palates craved the taste of human flesh. Then we altered our casus belli, and killed to bind in bondage the surviving victims of our onslaught. Then we learned to kill in order to take from the conquered their possesions, and then to turn them loose to produce more. Now we kill to force the conquered to purchase our products.

When the bull ape made his kill he stood over the body of his victim and uttered a roar of triumph. Today we build bronze statues to the big killers of men.

It was once said, so we are told, "Blessed are the peace-makers." And something snapped in the wicked little brains of the politicians and priests; and they hung the one that said it.

"Millions of years ago," we are told, "mighty lizards, the largest land animals ever known, roamed the lands of the present United States. Some of their monster bodies were 50 to 75 feet long, but their brains were no bigger than your fists. Long, long ago they disap-peared, exterminated by other animals with larger brains and smaller bodies."

They are gone, never to return. Only their enormous bones are found, that record their past existence. They were "exterminated by other animals with larger brains and smaller bodies." Such is the Law of Evolution, coming down through the ages—the development of larger brains, that slowly but surely exterminate the monsters with smaller and more brutal brains. This is, the Law of the younger world; this is the Law of today. As the brains of the race develop, the monster brutes disappear. For centuries there may be no apparent progress. Then, suddenly, one of the world's great epochs appears—a transition period in which Evolution, gathering all its accumulated forces, bursts forth into Revolution. Some of these great epochs are within recorded history; countless more of them are lost in the vast silence of the voiceless ages. It is into one of these great epochs—these transition periods—that we are now entering. The evidence of this is on every hand. Brains are once more battling with the brutes. The New Man with more brains is here, challenging the monsters of the present the right to devour the earth. These monsters, like their prototypes, the lizards of long ago, have lived their day. They are utterly worthless and useless to the oncoming race with more brains. The New Man with more brains has no use whatever for the monsters that despoil and devour the earth. The New Man with more brains wants the earth for himself, and he is going to take it. The New Man with more brains hungers for the beautiful, not the brutish; the lovely, not the lizardly. The New Man with more brains has visioned a world of Peace and Plenty, of Comfort and Comradeship, in place of a world of War and Wretchedness, of Masters and Menials.

The monsters that prowl and pollute the earth must leave. Their presence makes the earth filthy and foul; and the New Man with more brains demands that the earth be clean and sweet. And so the Monsters of the Present, like the Monsters of the Past, are going to be exterminated, they and all their Dark Age myths. The New Man with more brains is not only going to work for Himself, but also think for Himself. These "mighty lizards" of the past—"they disappeared, exterminated by other animals with larger brains." Prepare to join them, ye Monsters of the Present, ye devourers of human flesh and blood, ye war-demons and exploiters that befoul the earth! The New Man with more brains is here, and your kind is doomed.

NATURE is not purposely cruel nor wanton in her ways; Nature is simply law. In the slowly cooling process of the earth a great fissure breaks—the earth totters and trembles—the equilibrium must be regained or all is lost, and in the fearful shock man is crushed. Great vacuums occur, and Nature rushes her giant forces to fill the breach, and before the terrific tornado tumbles the habitations of man, and he is buried beneath. Nature did not intentionally send the earthquake and storm to kill and destroy—Nature simply followed law. The death and destruction is not the burst of passion of an angry deity, it is not the punishment of sin. Neither will prayer or incantation save us in the presence of these terrific processes of Nature. Only by our own efforts can we hope for protection. We may learn to build our habitations more secure, to move away from the earthquake zone, and thereby lessen these calamities that overtake us. This is all we mortals can do.

And yet how infinitesimal appear the ravages of natural law when compared to the wanton slaughter we inflict upon each other! There is not a day passes but that we crush and kill thousands more of our brothers and sisters, and their babies, than are crushed by the elements. This we can stop. These calamities are the only awful things we should fear, because these destroy both soul and body. The storms and shocks of nature we can bravely meet; we can clasp our hands together and face destruction, if need be, with never a fear, and with souls as clean as human love can make them. But the blackhearted torture and slaughter in the mills of mammon—the agony and death on bloody battlefields— these debase us and make us unclean and unworthy.

Among the Japanese there is an ancient custom, solemn and stern. A Japanese father takes his boy, at a certain age, and, in the twilight of the darkest night of the month, leads him to the top of a mountain. There, with a loaf of bread and a jug of water, the father leaves the boy. All night long, in the solitude of Nature, the boy remains alone. The lesson being taught the lad is very simple and sweet. He must learn that there is nothing in all the universe to fear, save his own thoughts and his own deeds.

For my part I am glad that the Universe is run by law and not by miracles. I feel far more secure as I journey through life governed by immutable law than I would were I floundering about subject to the fancy and caprice of an epidemic of miracles. The large and varied assortment of sorceries that our ancestors taught and believed would not suit me at all. I am glad that they never happen since public schools and newspapers came into vogue. Whenever a great man was born into the ancient world, it was generally a god that was his father. I wouldn't like that—if a bright child comes to my home I at least want the credit of being its parent. Of course this kind of a miracle might have been a convenient thing at times. If the husband took a trip, for say a year or two, and came back and found an addition to the family, it doubtless hushed a big scandal if the good spouse could charge it to one of the gods. But all the same I am glad that it doesn't happen any more—I am glad that day is past.

Those old miracles made lots of trouble—in fact they perpetrated many a thing that would be classed with the criminal and insane today. There was Abraham, and the notion he had that Jehovah wanted him to slaughter his son Isaac as a sacrifice. It was only a miracle that saved Isaac. It's a good thing that Jehovah doesn't crave human sacrifices any more—it takes all the blood we can spare these days to keep Mammon on its throne. And yet we have moved along quite a bit since Abraham's day. Let us be thankful for that. Suppose some present day saint with long hair and whiskers should wander along the road leading his son by the ear and flourishing a big knife, and singing psalms about how he was going to butcher the boy and roast his remains to the glory of his god. He would not go very far. He would be run in by the police. He would land in an insane asylum, and wear a straightjacket every time he showed symptoms of his religion getting the best of him.

Then there was Balaam and his charmed donkey, that

carried on a conversation with an angel. I am glad those things do not occur any more. If every mule hitched to a load of corn saw angels on the way to town and stopped to gossip with them, the farmers never would get home in time to do the chores. If a farmer nowadays does get back home along towards the next morning, and tells his wife that he met an angel in town, there's trouble, and I am glad of it. It's a good thing that miracles are discredited today, and that the women are wiser than they used to be. It helps keep the old man steady.

Then there is the story of Hezekiah and his boil. Hezekiah was awfully sick with his boil; he thought it was going to kill him, and so, in order to convince him that he was going to get well, a juggler induced Jehovah to pull the sun back ten degrees. It would appear as though it would have been an easier miracle for Jehovah to have cured the boil than to have moved the sun, but the gods in those days did all sorts of queer things. I am glad they have quit it. It's a good thing that this method of curing boils isn't practiced any more. If the solar system was shoved around in such a reckless manner every time anybody had boils the calendar would soon be so mixed up that the common people would not know when rent day came around. If Hezekiah were living today he would be told to go to a doctor with his boil, and not to be meddling with the sun.

At one time it was a serious question with the doctors of divinity as to whether Adam had a navel or not. Some of the reverends held that as Adam was created full grown and had a sound set of teeth from the day he was made, that he needed no navel and therefore had none. Others held that he had one, even though he had no use for it. They said he would have looked queer without it. The question never was definitely settled. It was simply pigeon-holed by the doctors of divinity.

The question as to whether or not unbaptized infants go to hell still looms up at times in Presbyterian circles. Their confession of faith declares that they do. Jonathan Edwards and Cotton Mather said that hell was full of damned babies, and advocated that the Quakers, who did not believe this doctrine, be hung. They were.

Then there is the Calvinist doctrine of predestination, or foreordination, or foreordained damnation. Synods of Presbyterian preachers have argued for years over the blessed gospel of God having selected, before their birth, a chosen few for eternal bliss, and, to his own goodness and glory, having damned to endless torment the vast majority of the human race.

The doctrines of infant damnation and foreordination are still matters of dispute. Like the question regarding Adam's navel, they ought to be settled. Such questions are more vital than bread and butter. Whether Adam really possessed a navel, or whether he had a paunch as smooth as a brass doorknob, or whether the doctrines of election, infant damnation, etc., were started by a lunatic or a spook, are far more important among the theologians than the question of arranging our social system so that those who create the wealth shall have it.

Paying homage to masters and reverence to myths

have proved a splendid charm to hold slaves in submission. It makes them forget their own miseries. It seems strange, but human beings do things in this world that would appear foolish, if other animals did them. Man is the only creature that is superstitious. You could not frighten a monkey about going to hell when he died. You could not make a monkey believe that an overproduction of the food supply should cause a panic and make him go hungry.

Perhaps the reader has heard the story of the traveler in Africa who found a forest of cocoanut trees inhabited by a tribe of monkeys. Cocoanuts were growing there in such abundance that the monkeys could not begin to eat them all. It was a case of the biggest kind of overproduction, and, according to the civilized Christian's school of political economy, the monkeys should have been starving—should have been afflicted with the worst sort of a panic. But the monkeys were not suffering from hunger. They were not having a panic—they were having a picnic. But they were only monkeys, and did not know anything about the political economy of civilized Christians. They did not know anything about going to hell when they died if they did not believe some creed. They had no creed—they did not know a thing about the inspired injunction that declares "servants, be obedient to your masters." They did not have any masters. That is why they were having a picnic instead of a panic. They had no saints to tell them that by suffering in this life they would stand a better chance of enjoying themselves after they were dead. They had never heard of the pious St. Eusebius, who carried two hundred and sixty pounds of iron on his body in order to please God. He was on his knees for years. He could not walk; he could barely crawl. He never smiled; he only prayed. His body was a mass of sores and bruises and filth. His soul was the only thing about him that was in first-class order.

The monkeys had never heard of St. Barnabas, who had a sharp stone inserted into his foot. It hurt awfully, but Barnabas would not let anybody pull it out for fear of the wrath of God. He slept on a bed of thorns, and fasted until he became a holy skeleton. You could not induce a monkey to do these things. Monkeys do not long for holiness that bad.

Then there was St. Hilarion, who was a wonderful performer of miracles. One of St. Hilarion's miracles that is regarded as a special proof of his piety was performed upon a young woman, who was despised by her husband because she bore him no children. She paid a visit to the cavern where St. Hilarion held forth, where the saint, we are told, prayed for her long and earnestly. And sure enough, his prayer was, in due time, answered.

Monkeys know nothing of the days when fables were revered and facts were outlawed, when doctors of delusion were the teachers and scholars were burned at the stake, when the gods were continuously at work upsetting the laws of nature.

The priests of the different deities were all charmed. The Christian saints finally established their reputations by outclassing the pagans in miracles. Among these was

Saint George, the patron saint of England, and the stories told of him were once as firmly believed as the story told of Christ driving the devils out of a man and sending them into swine. The evidence is the same in both cases. It should not be at all difficult for those who accept the virgin birth to believe the miracles and wonders told of Saint George. The performances of this saint are given to us as follows:

In the kingdom of Libya lay a great city, Selene, which was in the power of a monstrous dragon. Every day the people had to give this dragon a young and tender maiden for food. These maidens were selected by lot, and one day the lot fell to the only daughter of the King. The King was mightily grieved and offered the people half his treasure if they would offer a substitute.

The people, however, would not listen to it. "It is your duty, as it was ours, to bow to the choice," said they. "Lead forth your daughter or we will burn you and your palace with fire!"

Then the King's daughter put on her most precious robes, decked herself with pearls and gems, and went alone out of the city gates after a heart-breaking parting from her father. Weeping, she walked to the spot where the dragon waited for his daily food.

Just before she reached the fatal spot, however, a strong, handsome knight galloped up on a snow-white horse. He bore a white shield with a blood-red cross and over his helmet hung a golden dove with spread pinions. "Be of good cheer!" he said to the princess.

The dragon lifted his horrid head, saw the knight and

rushed at him. The knight made the sign of the cross, couched his lance, and smote the dragon such a blow in the neck that the monster rolled over completely stunned.

"Hasten to him!" said the knight to the Princess. "Fear not! Put your belt around his neck." She did so, and the bleeding, groaning dragon followed her like a little dog.

When the people saw the dragon approaching the city, they wailed with terror and prepared to flee to the mountains. But the knight cried: "The Christian God hath sent me! Believe in Christ, and I will kill the dragon!"

The king and all his people fell on their knees. The knight drew his sword and killed the monster. Then he baptized the people, who until then had been pagans. We are told that 30,000 became Christians in one day.

The knight refused all reward. None of the king's treasure could tempt him. "Give it to the poor!" said he. The king did so, and with the remainder he built a great cathedral. When it was finished, there came a wonderful sign from heaven. A spring of pure water poured from the altar in never-ceasing flow, and the water had the power to cure all sick Christians who drank it.

But because the king and his daughter and all the people praised the knight, and tried continually to lavish wealth and luxuries on him, he would stay no longer. This was because he had taken the vow of poverty and had given himself to the mission of spreading Christianity through the world. For this he had left his rich home in Palestine, where his father was Margrave.

So he bade the people of Selene farewell and went to the chief place of idolatry, where the Emperor of the Heathens had proclaimed a great tournament. He entered the lists and announced: "I am George, a knight of Palestine, and I have come to fight for Christ!"

"Join us, rather!" said the emperor. "You shall have lands and men from me, if you will but renounce your God and worship our deity, who is Apollo, God of the Sun."

"I will answer you tomorrow," answered George. He rode away and sought shelter for the night in a poor hut occupied by a widow and her little son, who was paralyzed. "Will you believe in Christ if I cure your son?" asked the knight. She kneeled to him and promised she would believe. Saint George then stooped over the boy and kissed him. At once the child arose, cured.

The widow picked up the child and carried him through the city. When she returned, followed by a great throng, there was another celestial wonder for them to see. The wooden pillars of the hut had become a great green tree which arched great branches with bright leaves and lovely flowers over the house. Thousands of birds sang in the branches, and all around was the odor of roses and violets.

The news of the wonder reached the Empress, and she went with her lady-in-waiting to see it. As soon as her eyes beheld it, she, too, fell on her knees and acknowledged Christ. A radiant cloud floated into the hut and hung over her head as the knight baptized her and saved her soul.

The next day the Emperor gathered all his nobles and all his soldiers and waited to see Saint George offer a sacrifice to Apollo. The knight arrived, followed by a multitude, among them the little boy who had been cured. "Where is the god to whom you wish me to make sacrifice?" asked Saint George.

"He is in the temple!" answered the Emperor. "We will go there now."

"I do not wish to go there!" answered the knight of the blood-red cross. "Let him come to me!" He gave a rod to the boy and told him to go to the temple and command Apollo to follow him. "If he will not obey, beat him till he yield!" said Saint George.

The Emperor and all his nobles laughed aloud; but all at once they saw the huge brazen god Apollo walking toward them, followed by the lad, who was lustily beating him with the rod. Before the amazed heathens could utter a word, Saint George commanded the idol: "I order thee to confess the true God!"

Thereupon the brazen god bellowed dreadfully and said: "Thy God is the true God, and Christ is the Son of God!"

"Then away with thee, accursed one!" shouted Saint George, and the god of brass instantly burst into millions of fragments and vanished.

The Emperor and the nobles, instead of being converted by this wonderful sign, became wild with rage. They seized Saint George and carried him to a wheel that was armed with double-edged knives. But when they tried to force him into it, the wheel burst and killed many heathens, but left Saint George uninjured.

The Emperor then ordered men to fill a great cauldron full of molten lead. Into this they tossed Saint George, but the fluid metal did not harm him any more than so much water.

The Emperor's sorcerers then made a death-drink of evil herbs picked on murderers' graves at midnight, the poison of adders, and other such ingredients. Saint George made the sign of the cross over the brew and drank it. When the sorcerers saw that it had done him no hurt, they fell prostrate and became Christians.

Enraged beyond all reason, the Emperor cried that the knight must be killed at once. Then his wife prayed for him and acknowledged that she, too, had become a Christian. At these words the Emperor frothed at the mouth. He ordered the Empress scourged till she died under the lashes.

Then he had Saint George tied to the tail of a horse which dragged him through the streets all day long, and in the evening when the knight was dragged back into his presence, he struck off his head with a sword.

That naturally ended Saint George's earthly career.

But Jehovah was on the job and avenged his death. He poured fire and brimstone down from heaven, and burned up the Emperor, his palace and all his heathen followers.

They are now broiling in hell.

Thus endeth the Gospel according to Saint George.

Monkeys know nothing of such miracles and wonders.

Monkeys manage to get along without mysteries or miracles, masters or saints, poverty or war. The jungle knows no such spot as the industrial sections of our modern cities, where human beings are existing in such abodes as respectable farmers would consider unfit for swine Here criminals are made faster than society can build prisons to contain them. For we create our criminal class, just as surely as we create the diseases that kill our babies, make invalids of millions, and send the vast majority to early graves. It is very simple, this process of making a criminal. Pick the most conscientious man in your community. Let him go hungry three or four days, and the criminal instinct will begin to creep up his system in spite of his conscience. Let his wife and babies suffer hunger but one day, and if he has any red blood in his veins he will steal as readily as the "unsaved" product of the slum. In these congested and insanitary slums of human multitudes the deadly germ of the great white plague finds its most fertile breeding spot, to be scattered all over the land. Here the lives of women and young girls are ground into profits, that others, whose dainty hands were never soiled by useful work, may revel in splendor. And the churches teach all manner of salvation for the poor except to quit plundering them.

Is this present world, with its wars of exploitation and its wrecks of souls, its sweatshops and its child labor, its degradation and poverty, its women driven to sell their bodies in order to live, its filth-bred diseases and countless more abominations, and with the iron heel of plundering wealth driving the race deeper and deeper in the mire—is all this hideous nightmare supposed to be anything at all like the kingdom of heaven on earth that Jesus dreamed of?

All the varied confessions of faith that bind the brain and hold the masses apart have nothing at all to do with the right relation of men to each other. They have nothing to do with the gospel of Brotherhood and Peace. They have nothing to do with the injunction that men should love each other and not hate each other. Who with clean soul can think that the Power that guides the Universe can care whether a man be a Jew or Gentile, Agnostic or Atheist, if that man is true to every impulse of human love and justice? When the religion of Love and Justice and Human Brotherhood shall touch the heartstrings of the race every discordant creed will be swept away, and the rapturous music of a united race will rise in full chorus throughout the world.

Seeking somebody or something to cringe and crawl to; some holy humbug's toe to kiss; some sceptered scoundrel to shed his blood for; some myth to mutter mummeries to; something, anything, stick, stone or spook, to prostrate himself before—such has been the common affliction of the common people. That in all the world's history there never was a ruler that did not exploit him, or a reverend that could get any of his gods to answer prayer, has not appeared to worry the average man a particle. Servility and superstition have been dearer to him than the needs and desires of his own flesh and blood. He turns over the larger part of all that his toil and sweat produce to keep the powers that plunder and humbug him in luxury. Yea, he deserts his **family** and sheds his blood to the glory of the plunderers. For this the ruler dubs him a hero, and the reverend promises to see that his soul is saved.

What are the poverty and privations, the sufferings and heartaches, the deadened love and longings of wife and children compared to the flattery of prince and fairy tale of priest? What a strange world it would be if the common people should get up from their knees and stand erect and declare themselves the equals of anybody that walks on two legs! And how wicked it would appear if they discarded the sticks and stones and spooks and adored themselves and their wives and children!

And yet, O Man, to this freedom of body and brain, the Spirit of Nature, the common Mother of us all, whose bible is an open book that all may read if they but will and not err, is calling her children.

Chapter VIII

A S to the Christian writings of the first and second centuries, Dr. Westcott, the Protestant commentator, says: "A few letters of consolation and warning, two or three apologies addressed to heaven, a controversy with a Jew, a vision, and a scanty gleaning of fragments of lost works, comprise all Christian literature up to the middle of the second century." The reputed sayings of Jesus, including his Sermon on the Mount, were not originally in writing. They were preserved by tradition, easily subject to alterations and additions. Dr. Westcott calls it "the dark age of Christian literature."

The reader will note the historic conclusion of this, viz., that nearly all of the so-called inspired writings found in the New Testament were originated generations after Jesus and his disciples were dead.

No wonder that Christianity depends upon faith alone. Its entire structure is built upon credulity, not evidence. For two hundred years there was no New Testament.

Then began the conspiracy to completely crush the

movement that proclaimed human brotherhood as the only salvation, and the creating of the institutional church. Roman priests wrote "revealed" gospels by the wholesale, reputing to Jesus the myths of their own imagination. Many of these gospels were so ridiculous that even the Council of Nice discarded them. Some of them are still extant. Also, fortunately, there still exists a number of writings testifying to the revolutionary teachings of the first followers of Jesus.

The clergy have ever been as Mosheim, the historian, describes the priests of the latter part of the second century: "They deemed it not only lawful, but also commendable, to deceive and lie for the sake of piety."

And what manner of men were these liars to whom we are indebted for our believe-or-be-damned religion? History affirms that Origen, one of the "inspired" authorities to whom we are indebted for a large part of the contents of the New Testament, declared that the sun, moon and stars were living creatures, endowed with reason and free will, and occasionally inclined to sin; he was not certain whether their souls were created at the same time with their bodies, or existed before, nor whether they would be released from their bodies at the end of the world or not. Lactantius taught that demons entered men through the viscera, but that the sign of the cross would drive them away. Gregory the Great preached that volcanoes were the entrances to hell. St. Thomas Aquinas said that diseases were the work of the devil. (We know now that they are caused by the Capitalist system, that creates insanitary conditions, poisoned food and filth.) All of the "inspired" priests who arranged our creeds believed in miracles, witchcraft and demonology. And for centuries the multitudes have looked up to these ignorant ancients and taught their children that they must "believe or be damned" all the fables written into the New Testament.

This does not deny that scattered throughout the gospels can doubtless be found some of the sayings of Jesus. Critics generally admit that the Sermon on the Mount, or at least portions of it, is traditionally true. It can be traced back to the first century, and was the only gospel message from Jesus that his first followers possessed. But all the dogmatic conceptions of after years, the doctrines of immaculate conception, the trinity of gods, paradises and perditions, are pure inventions of the Roman priests. These were constructed in order to transform the gospel of fraternity and freedom and peace into a religious system that upheld the ruling and robbing classes and enjoined upon the slaves submission to masters and servility to kings.

The Christianity that the world has followed after for all these centuries is nothing at all but a clumsy revamping of ancient Roman paganism, with Jesus, the simple-hearted proletariat\ and lover of humanity, made into a pagan god, a royal Emperor sitting on a throne.

I was taught the most despicable brand of Christianity when a child—the Christianity promulgated by John Calvin, maniac and murderer. The conception it gave me of God was something fierce. I can see the picture yet. The God of the Presbyterians looked like a big plug-ugly with a club in his fist. To my childish mind Jehovah was a fearful fright. Nor have I ever changed my opinion of him. He was no more to be admired than a Calvinist preacher. He sat on a gold throne with a gold crown on his head, with flocks of feathered angels, like buzzards, circling about him. A short distance from the throne was an immense hole that you could look into, and away down at the bottom was the blazing brimstone pit. From this horrible pit issued the screams and shrieks of the eternally damned. Men, women and little children, even babies, were enduring unutterable agony in the Christian hell. About three out of every four that died in the town where I lived went there. A fine picture to paint on the mind of a child.

And then one day the light came. I discovered that all this savagery was a lot of lies conceived in an age when slaves were held in awe by fear and superstition. Rebellious slaves were not only brutally beaten and put in chains, but were also told that there was a fiercer fiend in the skies than their earthly masters, who would broil them for all eternity if they did not submit to the ordained powers that be. Of course, the masters professed belief in this religion. It is an easy matter for the rulers and robbers to believe anything that is to their economic interests, and nothing in the world so elegantly supports their economic interests as a religion that teaches servants to be contented with their lot, and that keeps them alarmed about their precious souls.

I would that I could make all the robbed and outraged workers of the world realize that the rulers' god is created in the image of the ruling class. I would that I could make them realize that all the varieties of religious doctrines are only so many snares to keep the workers divided, and that Love and Brotherhood is the only religion worthy the notice of a clean soul—the only religion that can make this earth fit to live in—the only religion that can save us in this world or wherever eternity may call us.

Rob a human being of economic security, and you stab every sweet sentiment within his breast. Without economic security, without assurance of food and shelter, the soul of man becomes a desert. Lost is every deeper sense of life; music and laughter are forgotten; art is unknown; and love starves and perishes. An outcast upon the earth, robbed of economic security, sinks with the brutes. Those robbed of economic security do not sing, do not dance, do not play. They are joyless, song-less, loveless. No sweet melodies spring from wells down deep in homely hearts, no fireside folk-lore gladdens the daily toil. All becomes black in the ashes of despair. The homeless and hopeless cannot sing. The slum calls forth no music, the herded tenement hears no symphonies touched by Apollo's golden strings. The old plantation darkey sang; he knew no worry of the morrow; hard though the labor in the fields, yet, when the night shades fell, and all through the long winter days, meat hung on the lowly cabin wall. He played his banjo then, and sang such melodies as never since have been brought forth in all our land. Today, chasing that mod-

ern phantom called a job, the darkey hears no sweet re-
frain. "Old Black Joe" and the "Old Folks at Home"
could never have been sung by souls broken on the wheels
that are grinding now; the lowly cabin, the warm fire-
place within, the meat upon the log rafters are gone;
and the darkey sings no more. The Indian once sang;
when the buffalo and deer were his, songs of sweet con-
tent arose from the tepees, songs of the wild wood-folk,
love songs, songs to the Great Spirit that gave the corn.
These songs of Indian folk-life are almost lost. An ef-
fort is being made to collect the old Indian words and
music, for, we are told by musicians, the world has missed
a precious treasure in these weird, native melodies. The
Indian sings no more; the fire of music has gone out; an
exile upon the beautiful, bounteous earth, he hears no
note, save the savage shriek of the mad money-master
in the soulless, songless land of plunder.

By the rivers of Babylon there is no song—there our
harps are hung upon the willows.

No heavenly deity is going to miraculously set things
right in this world; you must do it yourself, or it will
never be done. In the governing power of the United
States votes count, not incantations.

And it is right and just that this is so. Man on his
knees begging is a sorry sight. Man standing erect and
doing for himself is far better and nobler than this.

Man depending on prayers is worse off than a blind
horse in a stump patch. There is no telling which way
the creature will go. He doesn't know himself.

Whatever progress we have made has been in spite of superstition, not on account of it.

The sending of a heretic to hell, the threat of everlasting torture to anyone too intelligent to believe something that is not so, has ever been the trump card in the hands of the rulers and their priests. The soul-saving claim of the church is only a blind; the real object of the creed of Constantine is to make the masses servile to the plundering powers that be. "Servants, obey your masters," and "be ye subject unto the powers that be," have been written into the mouths of all the masters' gods, from the Jewish Jehovah to the Chinese Joss. "There is, strictly speaking," states C. A. White in his "Students' Mythology," "no state or national religion in China, but all forms of worship are tolerated, unless they are considered politically dangerous." Just so. It's the same in this country. It was the same in old Jerusalem, when the rebel Jesus was preaching his politically dangerous doctrine. That the priests have transformed this rebel into one of their royal gods that upholds class rule and exploitation and war, is the theological crime of the ages. And yet the trick was easily turned. All that was necessary was to keep the masses ignorant and in poverty. The priests attended to the first of these, and the master-class to the second. The workers can thank the priests and the masters for their age-long degradation and misery. They can thank them for the bloody wars they have fought and the sufferings they and their wives and children have endured. If it were not for the priests and the masters the workers could peaceably inhabit the earth and enjoy it. This they have thrown to the winds through the fear of a priest-made hell in the bowels of the earth, and the hope of a priest-made heaven above the clouds.

All of the gods that have come down to us since the days when the first barbarian chief chained a slave are alike in character. They are all bosom friends of the barbarian chief. They are all vindictive, savage and cruel. They all sit on gilded thrones, crowned despots of an enslaved universe. They all demand sacrifices of both men and beasts. Of these gods Jehovah of the Jews was no exception. He gloried in human sacrifice, as well as that of goats and sheep. He loved the smell of burning flesh and blood. It made him feel good. "And Noah builded an altar to the Lord; and took of every clean beast, and of every clean fowl, and offered burnt offerings on the altar. And the Lord smelled a sweet savour." (Genesis, chapter VIII, verses 20-21.)

Leviticus, chapter XXVII, verses 26 to 29 inclusive, gives the regular bill of fare for sacrifices to Jehovah. Verses 28 and 29 of this chapter include the sacrifice of human beings. King David hanged the two sons of Rizpah and the five sons of Michal as a sacrifice to Jehovah. You can read about it in the second book of Samuel, chapter XXI, verses 6 to 9. The 9th verse says "they hanged them in the hill before the Lord." Probably their remains were religiously roasted on a stone altar after they were duly hanged. This made a "sweet savour" for Jehovah.

Genesis, chapter XXII, verse 2, says: "And he (God)

said (to Abraham), Take now thy son, thine only son Isaac, whom thou lovest, and get thee into the land of Moriah, and offer him there for a burnt offering."

Jehovah, however, according to the "inspired" scriptures, was only joking with Abraham, and at the last moment, after Isaac had endured all the agony of a tortured mind, concluded that the smell of a roasting ram would satisfy him this time, instead of the smell of a roasting boy.

It did not go so well, however, with Jephthah. He also, like Abraham, feared this God Jehovah, and kept his promise and offered up his own daughter—his only child—on the altar. And Jehovah did not stop Jephthah. He calmly watched while Jephthah cut his daughter's throat with a butcher knife. He distended his divine nostrils when Jephthah laid his daughter's bleeding body on the altar. He took a good, long smell when the savour of the burning flesh of the girl began to ascend to heaven. (See Judges, chapter XI, verses 30 to 40.)

And yet people of today, who shudder at the sight of the ruins of the stone altar that still stands at Stonehenge, in England, where the old Druid priests offered human sacrifices, teach their innocent children to sing "Guide us, O thou great Jehovah!"

The difference between the ancient Druid God and the God of Christendom is only a matter of faith. Faith can make a man believe in any god or gods the priests tell about.

The creed of Constantine has for centuries held the workers of the world in mental and physical bondage. To believe that the books of the Bible are divinely inspired is to believe that every curse that has ever been put upon the race, such as slavery, serfdom, exploitation, child-labor, the degradation of woman, poverty, misery and war are holy and ordained of God. Jehovah is made to bless these infamies. The slave laws of the Bible are explicit, and admit of no misinterpretation. In Leviticus, chapter XXV, verse 44, Jehovah says that his followers—of the exploiting class—should buy and own slaves of the heathen. Upon the persons of these slaves, male and female, the masters can piously commit any outrage they please, from rape to murder. Jehovah doesn't care. The god that smiled as he smelt the blood of Jephthah's slaughtered daughter can stomach anything. And if the slave laws and the sacrificing laws of the Bible were holy when they were written, they are holy still. And if they are crimes now, they were crimes then. Jehovah put women, slaves and barnyard stock in the same category. He scratched this law with his finger nail on a tablet of stone and gave it to Moses. He said, "Thou shalt not covet thy neighbor's wife, nor his man-slave, nor his maid-slave, nor his ox, nor his ass," nor any of the rest of his livestock (Exodus, chapter XX, verse 17). The coveting of the women was as bad—and no worse—than the coveting of any of the other of the master's belongings. It was as bad as it is for a working man today to covet the full product of his toil. Oxen and asses and sheep and goats and wives and slaves were all lumped together; they were blessings bestowed by Jehovah upon his chosen few; and the chosen few were allowed to possess as many of these blessings as their means would allow. This shows Moses was inspired of God. So likewise was Mohammed when he wrote the Koran. So was Joseph Smith when he wrote the Book of Mormon. So was Shack Nasty Charley when he danced the ghost dance of the Modocs. They were all inspired, all on familiar terms with their gods. Mohammed saw God. Moses saw God. That is, as before mentioned, he saw him from the rear. Jehovah told Moses that he dared not let him gaze upon the dazzling splendor of his front view. It might kill him. "But," said Jehovah, "there is a place by me, and thou shalt stand upon a rock; and it shall come to pass, while my glory passeth by, that I will put thee in a clift of the rock, and will cover thee with my hand while I pass by. And I will take away my hand and thou shalt see my back parts; but my face shall not be seen" (Exodus, chapter XXXIII, verses 20 to 23).

It seems too bad that Moses could not have had a kodak with him and have taken a snapshot. It would be interesting to even have a hind view of the god that overran Egypt with body lice and other like plagues, and that finally butchered all the Egyptian male babies in order to bring Pharaoh to terms; the god that murdered the Midianites, old and young, male and female, and saved only the young virgins for the lust of his soldiers; the god that sent a brace of she-bears to tear to pieces forty-two little children, because they laughed at the sight of a bald-headed wizard; the god that dragged King David's wives into the streets of Jerusalem and had a company of rakes publicly outrage them, as a punishment upon David for having killed Uriah, in order that he might add Uriah's wife to his already overstocked harem; the god that made the sun stand still so that Joshua could make a bigger killing, that turned rivers of water into blood and inquisitive women into pillars of salt, that loaded obstinate fortune-tellers into the stomachs of big fish, that had angels stop and talk to donkeys, that never had his fill of blood until he had his own son slaughtered —the picture of this god of miracles and monstrosities, even if it were only his hind parts, as viewed by Moses, would add immensely to the world's collection of religious relics.   If inserted as a fontispiece in every Bible it might Christianize the heathen so completely that the Christians would not be obliged to go to war with them in order to make them willing to accept our Christian civilization.   We have pictures and images of Jupiter and Diana, of Mars and Juno, and other gods and goddesses of mythology; we have carvings of Isis and Osiris of the Egyptians, of Brahma of the Hindoos and Joss of the Chinese; we know how most of the gods appear, but, alas! of Jehovah of the Jews we have no likeness; we can only imagine him as described by some of the inspired writers; he absolutely refused to sit for his picture; he positively forbade having himself portrayed or carved in the very first commandment he gave Moses on the stormy summit of Sinai.   He said he was jealous of the rest of the gods—probably because they were better looking—and he did not propose to have any imitations of himself or them adorning Hebrew art galleries.

Jacob, the son of Isaac, once, we are told, had a wrestling bout with Jehovah that lasted all night. Jacob says he then saw him face to face. Jacob must have had a stronger constitution than Moses, as the sight did not kill him—didn't even make him sick, according to the record (Genesis, chapter XXXII, verses 24 to 30). On the contrary, such a husky heavyweight was Jacob, that, says the narrative, he managed to obtain such a powerful hold on Jehovah that Jehovah could not break away, even after he had twisted one of Jacob's legs out of joint. Finally, after forcing a blessing from Jehovah, Jacob turned him loose. This is another loss to the world. Jacob should have held on to him while he had him. He should have called for help and put him in a cage.

Travelers tell us that in the interior of Africa such wonders as these still occur. That is, if you believe what the natives say.

For centuries those who denied such stories underwent every hideous torture that the priests could possibly conceive. Their tongues were pulled out with red-hot pincers, their eyes were burned out with red-hot iron, their feet and limbs were roasted till they fell off over coals of fire, they were strung up by the thumbs and heavy weights attached to their feet, their bodies were broken on wheels, and if they did not recant the reverend fiends burned them at the stake. Simple-minded old women were hung and burned as witches, for did not this God Jehovah declare "Thou shalt not suffer a witch to live." (Exodus, chapter XXII, verse 18.) To force the race to worship this myth millons have been burned, hanged and flayed alive; and if it were not for the infidels that have fearlessly faced death in order to speak for truth and liberty, Jehovah and his crazed priests would still rule.

To the worship of Jehovah the Roman priests added horrors unknown to the ancient Jews. Their religion did not eternally damn those who had never heard of it, who did not believe it. In its declaration of faith, adopted at the National Rabbinical Convention of the Reformed Hebrew Church, held at Pittsburgh in 1885, are these words: "We reassert the doctrine òf Judaism that the soul of man is immortal. We reject, as ideas not rooted in Judaism, the beliefs both in bodily resurrection and in Gehenna and Eden (hell and heaven) as abodes for everlasting punishment or reward." It further declares: "We extend the hand of fellowship to all who operate with us in the establishment of the reign of truth and righteousness among men."

I am not writing a brief for the Hebrew religion; I am simply drawing a comparison. Jehovah of the Jews was cruel enough, but he never thought of the brimstone pit until the Christians put the final trimmings on him.

Some of the Jewish prophets are among the noblest souls that ever lived on earth. When I attack the Bible I do not attack these. I love them too well. Their poetic messages of peace and fraternity, when men should beat their spears into pruning hooks and their swords into plowshares, are treasures in the revolutionary literature of the world. But there are other prophets, in all lands, and among all races, and in all times, as great, or greater than these. Because these speak the truth they are hated by the bigots who declare that no one, unless inspired by their god, can speak or write as good and pure and wonderful words as found in the Bible.

Let us pause, for answer, and read the words of one of these, given to us within the memory of millions of the living:

"I believe in the gospel of Cheerfulness, the gospel of Good Nature; the gospel of Good Health. Let us pay some attention to our bodies. Take care of our bodies, and our souls will take care of themselves. Good health! And I believe the time will come when the public thought will be so great and grand that it will be looked upon as infamous to perpetuate disease. I believe the time will come when man will not fill the future with consumption and insanity. I believe the time will come when we will study ourselves, and understand the laws of health and then we will say: We are under obligation to put the flags of health in the cheeks of our children. Even if I got to heaven, and had a harp, I would hate to look back upon my children and grandchildren, and see them diseased, deformed, crazed—all suffering the penalties of crimes I had committed.

"I believe in the gospel of Good Living. You cannot make any God happy by fasting. Let us have good food, and let us have it well cooked—and it is a thousand times better to know how to cook than it is to understand any theology in the world. I believe in the gospel of good clothes; I believe in the gospel of good houses; in the gospel of water and soap. I believe in the gospel of intelligence; in the gospel of education. The schoolhouse is my cathedral. The universe is my Bible. I believe in that gospel of justice, that we must reap what we sow.

"I do not believe in forgiveness as it is preached by the church. We do not need the forgiveness of God, but of each other and of ourselves. If I rob Mr. Smith and God forgives me, how does that help Smith? If I, by slander, cover some poor girl with the leprosy of some imputed crime, and she withers away like a blighted flower and afterward I get the forgiveness of God, how does that help her? If there is another world, we have to settle with the people we have wronged in this. No bankrupt court there. Every cent must be paid.

"The Christians say, that among the ancient Jews, if you committed a crime you had to kill a sheep. Now they say 'charge it. 'Put it on the slate.' It will not do. For every crime you commit you must answer to yourself and to the one you injure. And if you have ever clothed another with woe, as with a garment of pain, you will never be quite as happy as though you had not done that thing. No forgiveness by the gods. Eternal, inexorable, everlasting justice, so far as Nature is concerned. You must reap the result of your own acts. Even when forgiven by the one you have injured, it is not as though the injury had not been done. That is what I believe in. And if it goes hard with me, I will stand it, and I will cling to my logic, and I will bear it like a man.

"And I believe, too, in the gospel of Liberty, in giving to others what we claim for ourselves. I believe there is room everywhere for thought, and the more liberty you give away, the more you will have. In liberty extravagance is economy. Let us be just. Let us be generous to each other.

"I believe in the gospel of Intelligence. That is the only lever capable of raising mankind. Intelligence must be the savior of the world. Humanity is the grand religion, and no God can put a man in hell in another world, who has made a little heaven in this. God cannot make a man miserable if that man has made somebody else happy. God cannot hate anybody who is capable of loving anybody. Humanity—that word embraces all there is.

"So I believe in this great gospel of Humanity.

" 'Ah! but,' they say, 'it will not do. You must believe.' I say, No. My gospel of health will bring life. My gospel of intelligence, my gospel of good living, my gospel of good-fellowship will cover the world with happy homes. · My doctrine will put books upon your shelves, ideas in your minds. My doctrine will rid the world of the abnormal monsters born of ignorance and superstition. My doctrine will give us health, wealth and happiness. That is what I want. That is what I believe in. Give us intelligence. In a little while man will find that he cannot steal without robbing himself. He will find that he cannot murder without assassinating his own

joy. He will find that every crime is a mistake. He will
find that only that man carries the cross who does wrong,
and that upon the man who does right the cross turns to
wings that will bear him upward forever. He will find
that even intelligent self-love embraces within its mighty
arms all the human race.

" 'Oh,' but they say to me, 'you take away immortality.'
I do not. If we are immortal it is a fact in nature, and
we are not indebted to priests for it, nor to bibles for it,
and it cannot be destroyed by unbelief.

"As long as we love we will hope to live, and when
the one dies that we love we will say : 'Oh, that we could
meet again,' and whether we do or not it will not be the
work of theology. It will be a fact in nature. I would
not for my life destroy one star of human hope, but I
want it so that when a poor woman rocks the cradle
and sings a lullaby to the dimpled darling, she will not
be compelled to believe that ninety-nine chances in a hundred she is raising kindling wood for hell.

"One world at a time is my doctrine.

"It is said in this Testament, 'Sufficient unto the day
is the evil thereof;' and I say: Sufficient unto each world
is the evil thereof.

"And suppose after all that death does end all. Next
to eternal joy, next to being forever with those we love
and those who have loved us, next to that, is to be wrapt
in the dreamless drapery of eternal peace. Next to eternal life is eternal sleep. Upon the shadowy shore of
death the sea of trouble casts no wave. Eyes that have
been curtained by the everlasting dark, will never know

again the burning touch of tears. Lips touched by eternal silence will never speak again the broken words of grief. Hearts of dust do not break. The dead do not weep. Within the tomb no veiled and weeping sorrow sits, and in the rayless gloom is crouched no shuddering fear.

"I had rather think of those I have loved, and lost, as having returned to earth, as having become a part of the elemental wealth of the world—I would rather think of them as unconscious dust, I would rather dream of them as gurgling in the streams, floating in the clouds, bursting in the foam of light upon the shores of worlds, I would rather think of them as the lost visions of a forgotten night, than to have even the faintest fear that their naked souls have been clutched by an orthodox god. I will leave my dead where nature leaves them. * * *

"While utterly discarding all creeds, and denying the truth of all religions, there is neither in my heart nor upon my lips a sneer for the hopeful, loving and tender souls who believe that from all this discord will result a perfect harmony; that every evil will in some mysterious way become a good, and that above all and over all there is a being who, in some way, will redeem and glorify every one of the children of men; but for those who heartlessly try to prove that salvation is almost impossible; that damnation is almost certain; that the high way of the universe leads to hell; who fill life with fear and death with horrors; who curse the cradle and mock the tomb, it is impossible to entertain other than feelings of pity, contempt and scorn."

These brave, beautiful words, these clean and sane visions of hope and love, fell from the lips of Robert G. Ingersoll. No priest or preacher will charge that he was "inspired" by their god. It was the savage that said, "Thou shalt not suffer a witch to live," it was the slave-herder that declared, "Both thy bondmen, and thy bondmaids, which thou shalt have, shall be of the heathen that are round about you; of them shall ye buy bondmen and bondmaids," that were divinely inspired. It was the war-demon that wrote, "Spare them not, but slay both man and woman, infant and suckling," that had hold of a god's hand when he inscribed it. And it was the theologian that penned the closing words of Mark that received his inspiration from Jehovah's throne —"He that believeth all these horrors and is baptized shall be saved; but he that believeth them not shall be damned."

CHAPTER IX

THE blazing brazen belly of Moloch into whose flames babies were flung by black-robed and black-hearted priests, while kneeling thousands sung hosannas to the monster, was no more infamous than the religion of the Christian God that is charged with begetting a son by a Jewish maiden and then having him sacrificed to appease his wrath and smell his blood; it was no more hideous than the religion that frightens innocent children with nightmares of the eternally damned.

Crawling to creeds and crowning plunderers have led the world to the shambles. Clasping painted ikons to his heart, the Russian peasant goes forth to kill or die for God and Czar; mumbling unanswered prayers the German worker bids farewell to wife and child, casts one last, lingering look on the green fields and hills of the Fatherland, and offers his life to the lust of God and Kaiser; with crucifix and amulet the French husbandman leaves the vineyards and orchards of France, leaves the joys of life and loves of hearth and home and plunges into mad slaughter for the God and masters on his back; with Bible in his breast the English factory slave crosses the channel to join the murder feast of God and King; and inspired by the same insanity the American patriot becomes prepared.

And behind them all is utter desolation; behind them all are broken, bleeding hearts of mothers, wives and sweethearts, of sobbing child and helpless babe; and all this awful holocaust, this unutterable agony of blood and tears, of death and desolation, that kings and masters may rule and rob—kings and masters that a despicable, lying creed has thundered for centuries were ordained by a god in the skies! The Christian God is so accommodating to the kings and masters that he leads to battle all the slaughtering butchers.

Does the world need a new religion?

I should think so.

It needs a religion that has no humbug or horror in it; a religion that spells human brotherhood, peace and plenty for all, and spells it in big, red letters.

A religion that knocks crowns and thrones and supreme courts into scrap.

A religion, that leaves no room on earth for any save comrades.

A religion of bread and butter, not of bunk.

A religion that recognizes that a hungry body cannot hold a sweet soul.

A religion that makes education and science, art, music and the drama, its creed.

A religion that declares that there is nothing to fear,

either in time or eternity, save injustice; nothing to bring joy, save service.

A religion that will not take away the hope of a hereafter to those who so believe, yet makes today as urgent for human happiness as all the stretch of the eternal years.

And what will we do with no ceremonies nor articles of faith, with no supplications nor incantations, with no sceptered god in the skies, no fork-tailed devil in a hell of fire?

Come with me—the beautiful earth that bore us, and the all-beholding sun whose golden rays call forth the myriads of mysterious life, and paint the hill and vale, the flower and leaf, the forest and stream, with all the prismatic shades, are calling you and me. There is no wrath of angry deities, no damned demons in earth or sun or sky. No—not even though in tempest's blast or earthquake, in lightning or flood, our passing lives are crushed. Nature is not filled with vengeance, no more than you or I, while journeying on, step unwittingly upon some struggling worm. The earth and sun, and satellites and stars, and all the living creatures of land and water and air, and the trees and vines, and the grass and flowers, and you and I, this is all there is. Bound by a throbbing, mystic tie we are one. Within us pulses life, and thought, and infinite desire. Gaze through the mightiest telescope the genius of man has built, and on beyond the visible suns shine countless more. No gilded thrones are found in all the boundless space where sit in fury these sky-gods of the priests—no demons waiting to seize the naked souls of heretics and drag them to a brimstone pit. Eternity is today, and today is eternity. The Soul of the Universe lives not in a gold-paved paradise with walls of jasper and gates of pearl, but lives in the yearning, wistful eyes of our brothers and sisters that princes have plundered and phantoms have frightened. Slavery and superstition are the only demons to fear, and Liberty and Love the only gods to adore. Peace and plenty is the only heaven, and war and exploitation the only hell. Knowledge and science are the only revelations that will aid us, and labor the only prayer that will be answered. The earth and all it contains is the heritage of all, and to deny the least of mankind his heritage is the only blasphemy there is. To crush a flower is brutal—to crush the hopes and longings of a human soul is murder.

Shall we look then for a world of perfection, of happiness unalloyed? No, not here—nor no matter where eternity may lead us. With another prophet of the present day who did not receive his inspiration from Jehovah of the Jungle, with Anatole France, I would say: "No—divine pity, which is the beauty of souls, would come to an end when suffering ended. That will never be. Moral evil and physical evil, unceasingly resisted, will unceasingly share with happiness and joy the empire of the world, as the nights follow the day. Evil is necessary. Like good, it has its spring deep in nature; the one could not be dried up without the other. We are only happy because we are unhappy. Suffering is the sister of joy; the breath of these twain passes over our harp-strings and makes them sound in harmony. If happiness alone blew on them, they would give out a monotonous, tedious sound, like silence. But to the inevitable evils, to those evils at once common and august which result from the state of mankind, there shall no more be added the artificial evils, which result from the state of our society. Men will no more be deformed by an unfair labor by which they rather die than live. The slave will come out of the ergastulum, and the factory no longer eat up men's bodies by millions."

And so for the frailties of mortals, that the churches so loudly condemn, while passing by such crimes as exploitation and war, we of the new religion must have charity. These are natural. But to the monstrosities of slavery and superstition—the chains made by a master-class and the goblins invented by a priest-class—we must show no mercy. These are abnormal. And we may well hope that human vices and frailties will become but petty things when men and women are surrounded by such environments that make virtue and honesty pay a better dividend than immorality and larceny. We may well believe, in the light of modern biology, that disease and suffering will grow infinitely less as we grow out of poverty and ignorance, as we approach that society when neither the profligate rich nor the degraded poor, furnish a vicious class. And some day, when economic freedom takes the place of jobs owned by a master-class, and sanity steps into our brains and drives out superstition, love shall stand by every cradle; and fear shall be banished from the tomb. We shall know then that the pains of child-birth are not the curse of a god, but are Nature's firm foundation of a mother's matchless love; we shall know that death is not a damnation brought about by the temptation of a snake, but is the returning of the soul to the source from which it sprang.   With the good Walt Whitman, we can bid our loved ones farewell—

"Ripples of unseen rivers, tides of a current flowing,
    forever flowing,
(Or is it the plashing of tears?   The measureless waters
    of human tears?)

"I see, just skyward, great cloud-masses,
Mournfully slowly they roll, silently swelling and mixing,
With at times a half dimm'd sadden'd far-off star,
Appearing and disappearing.

"(Some parturition rather, some immortal birth;
On the frontiers to eyes impenetrable,
Some soul is passing over.)"

We of the new religion cannot countenance slavery degrading the body, nor superstition poisoning the soul. And of this we can be sure; we can live and labor, we can love and hope.   And in such a world there must be no masters of any kind whatever—only laborers and lovers.

It is not the belief in a Universal Source of life that anyone should particularly object to; nor is the belief in the continuity of existence after death to be condemned. But the creed of Constantine, the Christian religion, that claims that the salvation of human souls depends upon blind belief in myths and miracles, and that dooms to eternal torment those whose brains revolt at these things, this creed, this myth, has caused already enough bigotry and bloodshed, ignorance and insanity in the world. A creed that pays homage to hallucinations, that declares that you must accept as inspired a book that outranks the Arabian Nights with its tales of sorcery and savagery, or a fire-eating fiend will snatch your soul as you breathe your last and plunge it into a lake of burning brimstone, this creed, this delirium of Dark Age priestcraft, deserves the utmost scorn and contempt. A religion that declares you must believe or be damned is a fraud on the face of it; it is a crime to teach it to a child. Such a religion has but one purpose—to hold the masses in servility. All the war-demons that sit on thrones are there by the grace of the god of this religion. All the masters of bread that have held the workers in bondage are kept in their seats by the help of the god of this religion. All the poverty and misery we endure are on account of the will of the god of this religion. All the wars of plunder are sanctioned by the god of this religion. And there is no such god. Earth nor sky does not contain him. He exists only in the imagination of disordered brains. He is as much of a myth as Mumbo Jumbo of the jungle.

As for its being a blessing to the common people of the world, the ones that do the work of the world, who wear no crowns and boast no titles, who have no superior "Sir" or "Hon.," or saintly "Rev." in front of their names, the creed of Constantine has proven itself a fraud and failure, a delusion and snare. The vast majority of the race have toiled their lives away in poverty and despair, have been led to bloody battlefields like sheep to the shambles; while the few have rolled in luxury, have led useless lives on stolen wealth. Every generation of workers has shed lakes of blood to hold in power the masters that despoil them; they have gone down on their knees to a Dark Age deity that says servants, obey your masters and be subject to the powers that be.

The tragedy of the world is that the masses believe that a god inspired the priests that wrote the Bible. If I should write such jimjams as the Bible tells about, and insisted that I was telling the truth, would the people declare that I was inspired? If I should assert that I went out in the brush one day and hid behind a rock, and there saw the hind end of a god wandering by, or that I had listened to a conversation between an angel and a mule, would the world of today acclaim me as a prophet of God? Or would it have me examined by a board of lunacy? If I should start down the road with a butcher knife in my hand, leading some boy to a pile of stones, there to be slaughtered and roasted as a sacrifice to a god, would I be glorified, or would I be run in by the police? If some young man's sweetheart in your community should be found to be pregnant, and her lover avowed his innocence, and the preachers should announce from the pulpits that a ghost was the cause of the girl's condition, how many, in your community, would believe the preachers? And yet these things, and more like them, according to the Christian religion, must be accepted, or you are a heretic headed for hell.

To accept a fact, that your reason approves, is sanity. To profess belief in a fable, that your reason repudiates, is superstition.

No creature on earth can be a Christian who does not renounce his reason. This is the necessary foundation of Christian faith.

Chapter X

TO BELIEVE in equality in the means of lfe, in justice and peace, requires no creed. Nor does a belief in the immortality of the soul need bloody sacrifices, or fearful threats, to prove it. This at least the Spiritualists and Theosophists have shown. Whether, or not, they have proven a future life, this can be said of them—they are every bit as good citizens as the Christians, and mentally they are infinitely freer. Charge their teachers with being 90 per cent frauds, if you will; even then they have the orthodox clergy beaten by 10 per cent. The orthodox clergy are 100 per cent frauds.

No—a man or woman can be good, can be kind, can be just, can work for a better world, can believe in a Universal Source of life, can believe that this life is but one phase of an ever-evolving life, and not depend upon priest-made books or creeds. But the religion that begins at the cradle with a doctrine of damnation; the religion that holds the race in subjection to the plundering and murdering powers that be; the religion that makes mankind get down on its knees to anything in earth or sky; for this mockery, this insult to humanity, I can find no words in the English language strong enough to express my contempt. With its fulsome promises if you accept it, and its miserable threats if you reject it, the creed of Constantine ranks as the most despicable of all the world's religions. The god that fills hell with honest heretics and heaven with those who do not dare to think, the god that satisfies his wrath with the smell of bloody sacrifices, the god that ordains kings, chains slaves, and outrages virgins, this god of wretchedness and ruin, is by long odds the choicest of all the deities or demons that the rulers and robbers of the world have ever been blessed with. No wonder the heathen gag at him. No wonder that Thomas Jefferson described him as "a being of terrific character—cruel, vindictive, capricious, and unjust." No wonder that Robert Blatchford has said of him, "do you think the bloodthirsty, vindictive Jahweh, who prized nothing but his own aggrandizement, and slew or cursed all who offended him, is the Creator, the same who made the jewels of the Pleiades, and the resplendent mystery of the Milky Way? Is this unspeakable monster, Jahweh, the Father of Christ? Is he the God who inspired Buddha, and Shakespeare, and Herschel, and Beethoven, and Darwin, and Plato and Bach? No; not he. But in warfare and massacre, in rapine and rape, in black revenge and deadly malice, in slavery and polygamy, and the debasement of women; and in the pomps, vanities and greeds of royalty, of clericalism, and of usury and barter—we may easily discern the influence of his ferocious and abominable personality. It is time to have done with this nightmare fetish of a murderous tribe of savages. We have no use for him. We have no criminal so ruthless nor so blood-guilty as he. He is not fit to touch our cities, imperfect as we are. The thought of him defiles and nauseates. We should think him too horrible and pitiless for a devil, this red-handed, black-hearted Jehovah of the Jews."

This is the god that places a crown upon the head of the Russian Czar and the German Kaiser and the British King, and all their like; for does not their Bible declare, "There is no power but of God—the powers that be are ordained of God—whoso therefore resisteth the power, resisteth the ordinance of God—and they that resist shall receive to themselves damnation."

Is such a creed fit for any but slaves?

It blesses every plunderer in the world—even Standard Oil.

It is this god, backed by his Bible, that made the German Kaiser, in his speech at Brandenburg, in 1890, exclaim: "I look upon the nation and people handed on to me as a responsibility conferred upon me by God, and that it is, as is written in the Bible, my duty to increase this heritage. Those who try to interfere with my task I shall crush." And again at Koenigsberg, in 1910, he said: "It was on this spot that my grandfather in his own right placed the royal crown of Prussia upon his head, insisting once again that it was bestowed upon him by the grace of God alone and not by Parliament or meetings or decisions of the people. He thus regarded himself as the chosen instrument of heaven and as such carried out his duties as a lord and ruler. I consider myself such an instrument of heaven and shall go my way without regard to the views and opinions of the day."

Unless we can discover something more respectable, to say the least, than this slave-herding, slaughter-smelling sky-terror of the Christians, we had better worry along as best we can without any god; better be humane and free with fearless doubts, than inhuman and servile with fearful frights. For my part, I would take the simple faith of the heathen Blackhawk, rather than kneel to the creed of Constantine: "The Sun is my Father, and the Earth is my Mother; and upon her bosom will I repose." I could not sleep of nights if I believed the monstrosity that dooms the most of mankind to such torture as only madmen could imagine. Perhaps, if some terrible crime were committed against a beloved of mine, I might in anger slay the one that did it; but I cannot conceive of anything that would make me blackhearted enough to thrust the soul of man or dog for all eternity into the fabled Christian hell. This Christian hell was dreamed by snakes, not by saints; it was visioned by insanity, not by inspiration. Priests of the patrician class of Rome—sexual perverts—sodomized sots, degenerates who had lost all claim to decency and manhood—these are the holy fathers that added hell and damnation to Jehovah's other horrors, that wrote the major part of the New Testament. No other religion on earth can boast such horrors. The human sacrifices offered to Moloch and Baal and Esus pale beside the contemplation of the everlasting fire and brimstone pit. Even the torture and agony of children crushed beneath the wheels of Juggernaut are as nothing compared to the burning forever and forever of unbaptized babies. Wild beasts, knew they the brutal lies poured into children's ears from Christian pulpits, would shun us as too low in life to associate with. No serpent's fang contains **anything** as venomous as the creed of Constantine. Let us banish the delirium of the savage priests of the savage past, and inscribe a new religion for the coming generations. Let us pick from the quarry of our language such stones as will give a firm foundation. Let us make a Bible of a few words—Justice, Liberty, Equality, Fraternity, Knowledge, Truth, Goodwill, Peace, Hope and Love—these be better than a thousand chapters of myths and miracles, and bloody sacrifices to an angry god. I think it would be fine if we of the new religion had upon our center tables a little volume, of less than a dozen pages, with one of these words upon each page, and upon the cover and fly leaf inscribed "Our New Holy Bible, Inspired by the Longings of the Human Heart." Such a Bible would appeal to the rational men and women of all the races and colors and tongues of earth. No one need renounce his or her reason to accept it. You could hand it to a little child without polluting its innocent soul with fear and superstition. Such a Bible in our homes would be a simple, sweet appeal to a better world to live in.

Justice—Liberty—Equality—Fraternity — Knowledge

—Truth—Goodwill—Peace—Hope and Love—is not this all-sufficient for both time and eternity?

Of what good is a religion that does not demand human brotherhood and peace?

Of what use is a gospel that does not kick kings off their thrones and exploiters off the people's backs?

What hypocrisy is this, that boasts its works of charity!

What a spectacle to behold upon the bounteous earth —millions of millions of plundered workers, victims of a social system that disinherited them before they were born, and a religion whose vaunted charity beggarly cares for a paltry few! With justice established on earth, charity would sneak away.

Jesus had nothing to do with the institutional church. He taught fraternity and freedom and peace, and the utter destruction of the master class. Take him, and Isaiah, and Nahum, and Malachi, and their kindred spirits from the Bible, and the rulers and exploiters and their servile priests can have the rest. The heralds of human brotherhood of every race and tongue, and no matter where their words are recorded, alone are worthy of our respect and love. Any man or any alleged god, no matter where recorded, that uphold a master and slave system of society, that glory in war, are only worthy of contempt. Any man, or any alleged god, no matter where recorded, that sanction polygamy—the vilest slavery and prostitution of woman—are despicable beyond words. The god of Abraham and David and Solomon is only fit for the pig-pen and kennel.

Had Jesus been a friend of the masters and their

priests he would not have been put to death. To him,
and to all the martyrs to brotherhood and peace, I gladly
pay the tribute of loyalty and love. Of him I have said,
and would repeat:

Once, long ago, came one who voiced the hope and
longing of the race with infinite love and passion. He
told of a Source of Life and Love that the world had
never known, of a common Father of a common humanity. He dreamed of a society strange and beautiful
—the Brotherhood of Man. His teachings were garbled
and doctored by the priests that wrote of him years
after his tragic death, yet, will we but search, the sweet
message that he taught, the burden of his soul, can be
found. He was not the tortured god of the dogmatic
creeds—he was the lowly carpenter, the brother of the
workers, the friend of man and the lover of woman.
"Call no man master," said this sweet-souled carpenter,
"for all ye are brethren." He cared naught for the traditions of the elders or the sacred books. With him it
was, "It is written so and so, but I say unto you something different." He wrote no book, he formed no
creed. He simply trusted that the words he spoke and
the dream he dreamed would some day find expression
and life in the soul of his class, the working class. For
the Father, he said, had anointed him to bring glad
tidings to the proletariat. He had come to set the captive free. Again and again his tender heart bled for
all who bore the heavy burdens, but with more anguish
than all for woman, the doubly chained captive. Had
he not defied the biblical laws that condemned the

woman? Had he not scattered the men who would stone her for that, which their very actions proved, they themselves had been guilty of? "I do not condemn thee, go thy way and sin no more," were new words—they are still new—to woman. And to Mary the harlot! She loved him much, because he, in all the woman-hated world, had called her his friend. Take all—all the conflicting words of the men who blindly tried to interpret this carpenter, and do with them as you will. I care not. The few preserved sentences that fell from his passionate lips—the scathing denunciation of the master class and the infinite love of the outcast—these are all I want. I turn from the dogmatic epistles half ancient Judaism and half Greek mythology, and I go again with the Peasant of Palestine down the beaten path to Bethany, where in an humble home lived Mary and Martha. There I can still hear the music of his voice, the simple story of love and brotherhood, as on the vine-clad porch he told it time and again. And the little children, how they swarmed to meet him! He was their comrade, their lover and the companion of their childhood. And now another voice, perhaps more stern than his, cries glad tidings to the woman and her child. It is the world-wide call of Socialism. Women, children, when every chain is broken, yours shall be the greater freedom, for yours has been the greater slavery!

And so, in the New Religion, that calls for brotherhood, and equal ownership in the means of life, that hurls from thrones and high places all the kings and exploiters and war-demons and gives back the earth to the common people from whom it was stolen, we shall ever cherish in our hearts the memory of the splendid souls who were faithful unto death in the cause of humanity—the pioneers of Peace on Earth, Toward Men Good Will. And we will hold in reverence no man, and no alleged god, and no priest-proclaimed inspired book, that puts masters on our backs, and blind beliefs in our brains. To allow anybody to assume that he is of better blood—of higher caste—than yourself, is servility; to allow anybody to make you believe that something is a fact that your common sense tells you is a fraud, is superstition; and superstition forges the chains of servility; and servility is an insult to Nature, the common Mother of us all.

Deep planted in the hearts of the masses is the longing for comradeship, for love and happiness. Nature put it there. And then, upheld by a cunningly devised fable that proclaims that "the powers that be are ordained of God," rise the hydra-headed monsters of mammon, drunk with the lust of pomp and power and plunder, and, with the poison of patriotism and the prayers of priests, the native love and longing is silenced in the mad fury of war. Away with them all—crowns and creeds, plunderers and priests, beliefs, bibles and bedlam, and back to Nature and Nature's common love of all! Back to Nature, of whom Goethe sang, "Her crown is Love. Only through Love can we come to know her. She puts gulfs between all things, and all things strive to be interfused. She isolates everything, that she may draw everything together. With a few draughts from the cup of Love she repays for a life full of trouble." This is faith enough, and hope enough, and religion enough, for all fraternal souls.

A sweet instance of the love and longing that Nature has planted in the hearts of the race comes to us from the battlefields of Europe. It is the story of a dying German soldier, who stretched out his arms to a passing French refugee woman, and asked leave to kiss the baby she was carrying in her arms. He was thinking of the baby he had left at home, in the arms of the sweetheart of his youth.

Let us drive from earth forever the monster powers that be, that make war and misery, and poverty, and with them the creed that proclaims as "inspired of God" the infamous injunction, "Let every soul be subject unto the higher powers. For there is no power but of God; the powers that be are ordained of God."

For a religion that puts monsters on thrones and masters of bread on the backs of the world's workers, I have the utmost loathing and contempt. I utterly repudiate the authority of any man or book that upholds these infamies. These have cursed the race long enough. Away with them, and the religion that supports them Let us build a New Society, and a New Religion. Let us start with a clean sheet. And let us see to it that no masters and no myths befoul the page.

EPILOGUE.

IT WAS Saturday night. Jimmy Burns, sitting in his small front yard, with his chair tilted back against the house and his feet planted in the rungs, had dropped his daily paper on the brown earth. There was no green grass—factory towns boast but little green around the long rows of cottages by the mills. It had become too dark to read, so, having absorbed a fair amount of the crimes and scandals and general doings of the outside world, he had lit his pipe and settled himself for rest and meditation. Jimmy's wife, with Katie and Johnnie and Annie and baby Jim had gone to the stores with the weekly check, and little would there be left in her purse when the necessaries and paltry luxuries were brought home. So Jimmy meditated. For all the years back since he and Maggie had pledged their troth and dreamed of happy days to come, he had gone through his evening course of meditation, in the winter time by the stove in the living room, in the pleasant summer months out of doors.

As the years went by and Jimmy's nature matured

182

under the hard school of much work and little pay, these meditations had changed their hue and the colorings grew deeper and darker. There was a time when his thoughts were as red as roses—he was younger then. Now they were more like the brown dirt in the cottage yard, where the grimy smoke had killed the grass. "It's a dreary world," said Jimmy to himself this Saturday night, "a dreary world for such as me."

He had repeated this same reflection time and again of late. When love was young and hope was strong he would have shuddered at such a thought. But Jimmy hardly recalled those days anymore. "It's a dreary world for such as me," he went on, "with nothing but work and eat and sleep, and then work and eat and sleep again. I'm like a beast bound to the treadmill—I'm no better than he. No, but I'm worse off than he is, for I can want for things and he can't. Now there's Maggie. I'm so glum these days I guess she thinks I don't have a thought for her any more. Well, it's an old saying that when poverty comes in at the door, love flies out the window. And yet I'd give my life to make her and the children happy. Look at her, poor soul! between doing all the work and raising the babies, and at times taking in washing when the mills are shut down, she's a sorry looking blossom to the bud she was when she married me. Her cheeks were blooming then and her laugh was as happy as a song bird. She's pale and worn-looking enough now. If I could but send her and the children away for a change! The banker and the landlord and the mill owners send their wives and children to the seashore and the mountains, and fill them with fresh air and life. And look at the things I want so much! A little home of my own up on the hill, not a rented tenement down here in the smoke, and books and a piano and such things that would make life worth the living. And what's the use of talking about all these things with wages barely enough for keeps, and the mills shutting down at times and no wages at all? I say it's a dreary world for such as me." And Jimmy knocked the ashes out of his pipe and wrapped himself in that mantle of despair that has been the only imperishable garment of the poor.

Maggie and Katie and Johnnie and Annie and baby Jim had returned and gone to bed, but the night was warm and Jimmy still dreamed on. At length he happened to look up the street and under the glare of the electric light he observed a man slowly coming down the walk. As the man drew nearer Jimmy noted that he seemed to be much interested in viewing the long rows of tenements on either side, every one of which being built so exactly alike as though to purposely torture the eye. "Must be a stranger in the town," muttered Jimmy, "the way he looks at the shacks. Maybe he's hunting for property investment." Finally the man came directly in front of Jimmy's yard and as he reached the gate he paused and spoke. "Pleasant night," he said, "and if you are not going to bed quite yet, comrade, and don't mind, I'll come in and rest a bit."

"Come along," answered Jimmy, and he arose and went to the front door and tiptoed into the cottage and brought out another chair. "Take a seat," he said, "and light your pipe if you have one, and make yourself at home." The stranger graciously accepted the hospitality extended, and presently both were comfortably seated and smoking their pipes.

"I should judge you do not live here," began Jimmy by way of an opening.

"No," replied the other, "and," he added, "I must say I am glad this is not my home."

"Traveling?" continued Jimmy.

"Just for tonight."

This remark appeared rather odd to Jimmy, but noting the stranger's neat, but not over-stylish apparel, he concluded that he was of the well-to-do class out in his automobile from some neighboring town.

"Then you do not like this burg," said Jimmy after a slight pause.

"No," answered the other, "for a workingman like myself this seems like a dreary place to live in."

"Like a dreary place to live in"—how like Jimmy's own meditations!

"But," continued Jimmy, after a little study, "surely you do not belong to the working class?"

"Oh yes," replied the stranger, "where I live all belong to the working class, whether the work be of brain or brawn. We have a beautiful place to live in. An eyesore like this street you live on would be torn down at once. We have lovely parks, and schools, and art museums, and public theatres and music, and we all spend part of the time in travel and at the seashore and mountains."

"At the seashore and mountains!" Jimmy felt a twinge at his heart-strings as he recalled Maggie's pale face, and his mantle of despair wrapped itself closer about him at the mention of parks, and schools, and art museums, and public theatres, and music, and his own soul-hungry bairns. And then the stranger went on describing the many charms and advantages of the city where he lived. He told of the freedom from disease, because of the perfect sanitary conditions and the absolute purity of the food supply, and dwelt especially on the wonderful effect, both mental and physical, the entire removal of worry and fear of want was working upon the people. Jimmy listened to it all with increasing wonder. Why, even the bankers and landlords and mill owners where he lived enjoyed no such life as this man described, for, when the pestilence and fever broke out in the crowded tenements, did not their poison reach the mansions on the hill? And the stranger told him it was *all the people* who enjoyed these things! "Such a pipe dream," Jimmy thought. And then, as the stranger looked hard at him, as though he wished to discover what effect his words had produced, Jimmy was suddenly seized with an inspiration.

"Say," he exclaimed, "could I move to your city and get a job?"

"Certainly you can," was the answer.

Jimmy's breath almost left him.

"I can start tomorrow," he simply said.

"But you cannot come alone," said the other.

"Of course not," replied Jimmy. "Did you think I

would leave Maggie and Katie and Johnnie and Annie and baby Jim behind?"

"No, I knew you would bring them," said the stranger, "but you must bring more than these with you, or you cannot come."

"Who else, then?" said Jimmy.

"You must bring ALL YOUR MATES."

* * * * *

"Jimmy Burns," cried a woman's voice from the window above him, "do you know it is nearly two o'clock?"

He awoke with a start. He rubbed his eyes—he looked at his side—but the stranger was not there. He could not realize he was alone, so vivid had the vision been. He gazed up and down the street—there was not a soul in sight—only the dull row of cottages and the dark outlines of the mills, with their chimneys silhouetted against the summer night sky. "What a dream!" he whispered, "and it was so real that it seemed true!" And he pondered over the words of the strange visitor, "YOU MUST BRING ALL YOUR MATES."

BEHOLD THE FUTURE !

Behold the Future
Rising from the ashes and agony of world-war!
The National is dead;
The INTERNATIONAL lives!
The plunderers and parasites are gone,
And their paid panders, the politicians and priests;
They are buried in the night—
The black and bloody night through which we passed.
The prince has perished;
The peasant has become the peer!
The warrior is a wastrel;
And the husbandman a hero.
The landlord and joblord are banished;
And there are no landless and jobless.
The chains that held Humanity in superstition and ser-
    vility are shattered;
The curse of creed and crime of caste are crushed;
And MAN only remains!
Sacrifice and supplication are scorned;
SERVICE is the only savior,
And LABOR the only prayer!
No more do fraud and fable fill the brain of the child;
Along the paths of TRUTH and SCIENCE the child is
    led.

The holy heaven and hideous hell have vanished;
Only the green Earth,
And the life-giving Sun,
And the lovers' Moon,
And the Stars in the bosom of eternity.
No deities to whom we cringe and crawl, no demons that
we fear;
These fled the hour we hurled the masters from our
backs.
None but Men and Women, and the beloved Children,
And the Spirit of Nature brooding over all;
And the Perennial Promise of sweet Peace and Plenty!

"The Life and Exploits

of Jehovah"

By HENRY M. TICHENOR

————o————

¶The Most Talked of Book of the Century—
Over 20,000 Sold the First Year
An Exhaustive and Amusing Collection of
the Ancient Legends Found in Biblical,
Apocryphal, Rabbinical and Mussulman
Writings of the Jungle God of the Jews

Handsomely Bound in Silk Cloth,
Price, Prepaid............................ *$1.00*

————o————

ADDRESS

THE MELTING POT

Pontiac Building   St. Louis, Mo.

SD - #0032 - 070825 - C0 - 229/152/11 - PB - 9781331311423 - Gloss Lamination